PRAISE

This book blends hard-earned SEAL leadership with practical mindfulness, offering honest lessons that apply equally at home and in high-pressure boardrooms. It's a grounded guide for anyone seeking clarity and purpose in a chaotic world.

> –Jason B.A. Van Camp, *Wall Street Journal*
> bestselling author and US Army Green Beret, Ret.

Jon Macaskill leads with uncommon integrity, and this book brings leadership back to what never changes—showing up with clarity, presence, and character in a changing world. It's a timely, grounded reset on what real leadership actually is.

> –Dr. Travis Hearne, USMC veteran, CEO,
> international best-selling author, and keynote speaker

Jon Macaskill cuts through the noise of the leadership and self-help world to remind us that leadership isn't about titles or intensity, but how we show up in the small moments, when no one is watching. This book goes beyond the SEAL label and calls leaders to lead with discipline, integrity, authenticity, and presence.

> –Dr. Theresa Larson, DPT, CSCS,
> USMC veteran, founder of Movement Rx

DIAL IN YOUR LEADERSHIP

Four Non-Negotiables for Leading with Clarity, Trust, and Purpose

Jon Macaskill

ISBN: 979-8-89079-476-5 (hardcover)
ISBN: 979-8-89079-474-1 (paperback)
ISBN: 979-8-89079-475-8 (ebook)

Jetlaunch Publishing

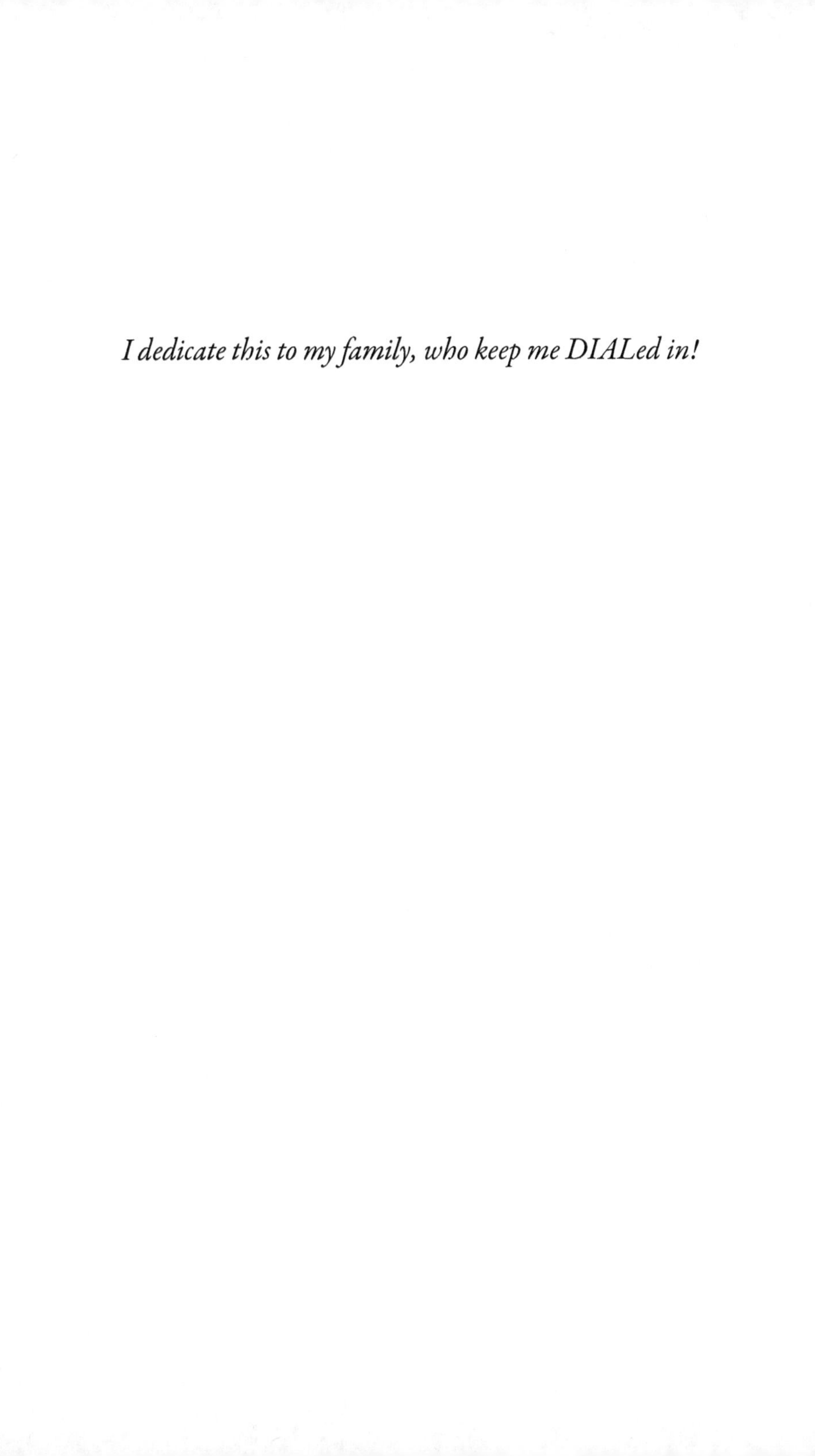

I dedicate this to my family, who keep me DIALed in!

Table of Contents

Introduction

Leadership. Man, I'll tell you what. You can't swing a dead cat these days without hitting someone claiming to be an expert at it or without hitting another leadership book being published.

Look, I'm not here to tell you I'm a leadership expert. (I'm not.) I'm also not going to say this is the leadership book everyone needs to read. (It's not.) But I do want to say that I've learned a lot about leadership in my life, and I'm continuing to learn more about it every day.

That said, this book is what I have learned so far.

Leadership isn't a title. It isn't rank. And it's definitely not about being the loudest person in the room.

Leadership is a responsibility—a weight you carry, by your choosing or not, because people around you need steadiness more than they need speeches.

There are no applause breaks. No highlight reels. Just moments when someone looks your way, silently asking, "What do we do?" and you steady yourself so they can be steady, too.

I had that truth drummed into my head on the morning of September 11, 2001. I was fresh out of the United States Naval Academy. An Ensign (first officer rank in the Navy) at Basic Underwater Demolition/SEAL training (BUD/S). I was standing at the threshold of the career I had dreamed about since high school.

Only months earlier, I had walked across a stage in Annapolis and received my diploma, my commission, and the handshake of the President of the United States, George W. Bush.

I still remember the exact moment when I heard the Twin Towers and the Pentagon had been struck. The images flashed across television screens: smoke billowing from every building, debris scattered through the streets of Manhattan, and then two towers that had once defined the New York skyline collapsing into dust. In a single morning, the course of history was permanently altered. We were young, and quite frankly, we were shaken. We were all wondering, *What does this mean? What do we do now?*

One of our instructors picked up on this tension and called us all together. He wasn't the senior guy, but he knew we needed steadiness. He jumped on a small stage and said, "Boys, people are calling this the second Pearl Harbor. Well, I can tell you this, as bad as Pearl Harbor was, it ain't shit compared to this! Your training just got a lot more important. You're training for war—a war that'll last decades! (He was right about that.) But you're in this together. You have a country to defend and a country that will support you."

These few words grounded us and bonded us together. We were brothers before we even entered the brotherhood.

That morning became the moment I understood that leadership is never about rank or bravado or holding a title. Leadership is the ability to bring clarity when chaos reigns, to build trust when fear corrodes it, and to remain steady when the ground shakes beneath everyone's feet.

The Seeds of Leadership

Though that leadership lesson from 9/11 stayed with me forever after that moment, I first learned it long before I ever wore a uniform. It didn't start with rank or achievement. It started quietly when no one was watching, and when someone handed me a responsibility that I wasn't sure I deserved.

For me, it began with pain right after my family moved from South Africa to the States. I landed in Ruston, Louisiana, with a foreign accent, the wrong timing, and a confusing academic start. South African school begins in January, so I'd finished only five months of first grade before being dropped straight into second grade in the US.

I struggled immediately. Eventually, I was moved back into first grade, and at seven years old, I was older than everyone else, so I was teased and labeled "the dumb kid."

That pain lit a fire in me—not the kind that burns everything down but the kind that pushes you forward. I didn't have the words for it then, but that moment planted early seeds of leadership. It taught me what it feels like to be on the outside, and later, it made me pay attention to the people quietly struggling in the back of the pack. It taught me that effort could close gaps that talent couldn't and that consistency mattered long before anyone noticed you. As I got older, that same fire started looking for a new place to burn, and that place became running.

Ruston is a football town through and through. Friday nights weren't just games; they were rituals. The whole town shut down. This was a place that produced legends like Terry Bradshaw, Fred Dean, and Ruston-born quarterback Bert Jones. Football wasn't just a sport; it was the standard. If you weren't wearing pads, you were background noise.

So, I tried football and basketball—and baseball. But I was painfully bad at all of them. I was too lank, too lean, and too unco-ordinated—more grit than power.

But I could run. And I loved to run.

My dad ran cross-country, and he was (is) my hero. I chased him the way only a teenage son can chase his father—wanting to match him, wanting to surpass him, wanting to understand him. Running became the first place where discipline and purpose made sense.

Track and cross country quickly became my first real love and my first real leadership training ground. As a freshman, our team went undefeated and won the state championship. The seniors who led us embodied everything I thought leadership was. They were steady, humble, and tough. And then, they graduated. Overnight, the team felt hollow. We were young, unsure, and very aware of the leadership gap.

One early morning during a training run for the next season, our coach pulled up beside me. (He used to run with us back then.) No speech, no team meeting, no buildup—he just said, "I'm making you captain this year," and drifted back into the pack.

I was a sophomore. I was not the fastest, not the strongest, and definitely not the loudest. My first thought was, *Why me?*

What I didn't realize at the time was that those early moments of being the outsider, of working twice as hard just to keep up, had prepared me for this. Leadership rarely shows up when you feel ready. It usually comes when someone else sees something in you that you haven't learned to see in yourself.

Being captain wasn't about pep talks or big moments. It was about showing up every single day. It meant picking up teammates before sunrise and dropping them off long after sunset because they didn't have cars, and I was privileged enough to have my own. It meant running the full route even when no one was checking. It meant paying attention: Who's struggling? Who's exhausted? Who needs encouragement? Who needs honesty? All skills I had unknowingly been practicing since grade school.

That season taught me one of the most important lessons of my life: people don't follow talent; they follow consistency. They follow the person who shows up, does the small things right, and pays attention when no one else does.

Those early lessons shaped who I would become. They built the foundation for the slowly forming dream of becoming a Navy SEAL.

The path wasn't linear. I was rejected from the Naval Academy the first time. That rejection hurt, but it also taught me resilience. I enlisted, reapplied, and eventually earned a Secretary of the Navy nomination and an appointment to Annapolis.

Each setback was its own invitation: Would you like to quit, or would you like to grow?

Is Leadership Harder Today?

If you listen to the conversations happening in boardrooms, on social media, or at leadership conferences, you'll hear a familiar refrain: "Leadership is harder today."

I don't believe that's entirely true. Leadership itself, at least the heart of it, in my opinion, hasn't changed much at all. People still need direction, trust, and stability. They still crave clarity when they're overwhelmed and honesty when things go sideways. They still look for someone who can hold the line when uncertainty grows.

What has changed isn't the fundamentals. It's the environment around them. We live in a world where every day brings more information, more opinions, more urgency, and more noise than leaders had to navigate even twenty years ago. The pressure isn't necessarily heavier, but it is more relentless. There are fewer pauses, less margin for drift, and less space to catch your breath.

Leaders today are moving through multiple realities at once. You're leading in person and through screens. You're balancing people's emotional needs with operational demands. You're expected to make quick, thoughtful, and inclusive decisions. You're judged not just by outcomes, but by tone, intention, and emotional awareness. And thanks to the digital age, every decision has a longer tail. Feedback doesn't take weeks anymore. It takes seconds.

However, calling this "harder" misses something important. It implies the answer is to grind more, push harder, or somehow keep up with the acceleration around you. In my experience, that's exactly the path that burns leaders out.

The goal isn't to match the pace; it's to not be controlled by it. The truth is simple: leadership isn't harder today. Leadership just requires more intentionality than ever before.

The leaders who struggle today aren't necessarily unskilled. A lot of them are *very* skilled, but they are overwhelmed. They're running hot, outpacing their nervous systems, responding to everything and reflecting on nothing. They're drowning in inputs: emails, texts, meetings, Slack messages, deadlines, and shifting expectations. They're losing sight of the centeredness their people need from them (and what they need for themselves).

The good news? We understand leadership better now than we ever have. Emotional intelligence isn't a buzzword anymore; it's recognized as a real strength. Vulnerability doesn't get you fired; it gets you trusted. We finally know what works. Leaders who listen first, speak with intention, and lead through influence are finally recognized for their strength.

We have more tools, more insight, more language, and more shared understanding. So no, I don't think leadership is harder. It's simply different. The pace has changed. The demands have changed. The landscape has changed. But the heart of leadership—showing up consistently with integrity, clarity, and presence—remains the same.

And that leads to the question every modern leader has to answer: How do I stay grounded when everything around me is accelerating?

For me, the answer eventually became clear. Through years in uniform and years out of it, I kept returning to four principles. These four qualities showed up repeatedly in leaders whom people trusted. Not perfect leaders—trusted ones. Not the loudest voices—the steady ones. The ones who brought peace into a room instead of chaos.

Those four qualities became the framework of this book: discipline, integrity, authenticity, and learning. Together, they form the DIAL model.

I call it the DIAL model because every warfighter knows this truth: you don't set your sights once and forget them. You dial in, adjust for wind and distance, and recalibrate. That's it—over and over. Leadership works the same way. You dial in your habits, your values, your presence, not because you're broken, but because you're human and the world keeps shifting.

These pillars are not theories. They're lived truths, tested in the harshest environments.

I've seen discipline keep men moving through Hell Week when cold and exhaustion tried to shut down their bodies.

I've watched integrity hold a team together after losing brothers in combat. It meant we had to speak truth in grief and still find the strength to carry the mission forward.

Authenticity rebuilt my life after my first marriage failed. I learned that admitting failure doesn't make you broken; it makes you believable.

And learning kept me growing even after I earned the Trident. Some of my best insights came from the youngest guys on the team. Today, some of my best insights come from my kids.

The goal of this book isn't that you admire my story. (A lot of this won't be my story.) It's that you uncover your own. Because leadership isn't reserved for executives or warfighters, it's something you're already doing, whether you realize it or not.

Maybe it shows up when your child looks to you for reassurance in the dark. Maybe it shows up when your employees wait for direction during a downturn. Maybe it appears in a crisis, when the people around you instinctively look for the most level-headed person around.

Leadership lives in these moments—human ones. Moments with no praise, no titles, and no guaranteed outcome. Moments when you decide who you want to be.

So, as you read, I invite you to reflect on your story. When was the last time someone looked to you for guidance? How did you respond? Which principles were present in that moment, and which ones weren't? Where do you notice the need to grow?

This book won't ask you to become perfect. It will ask you to become present, to notice how you lead when things are calm and when they aren't, and to see which instincts you rely on most and which ones tend to disappear under pressure.

Leadership is already within you. The question isn't whether you have what it takes. The question is whether you're aware of how you're leading in real time and whether you're willing to adjust when the moment demands something different.

The rest of this book is about those four things—not as some perfect checklist, but as real behaviors you can practice. How do they work together? When one gets out of balance, how do you notice it? How do you dial yourself back in when life pulls you off course?

That's where we begin.

1

A Brief Introduction to DIAL

When children in Flint, Michigan, began showing signs of lead poisoning, pediatrician Dr. Mona Hanna-Attisha suspected something was wrong and raised her concerns. State officials dismissed them. Data was withheld. She was accused of causing unnecessary panic.

But she didn't back off.

She collected her own data.

She analyzed blood lead levels.

She held a press conference against the advice of colleagues.

And she exposed the truth, forcing the State of Michigan to acknowledge the crisis and take action.

Her leadership wasn't about rank; she didn't have any. It was about moral clarity, discipline in the face of resistance, and the courage to act when others stayed quiet.

What Mona's story shows is simple: people don't follow a title. They follow clarity. They follow someone willing to do the hard thing when everyone else is comfortable staying quiet. The old "do what I say because I outrank you" model doesn't work anymore. (Did it ever?) It was built for simpler times, more predictable systems. Now it just breaks.

What organizations, teams, and communities need now are leaders who bring stability without rigidity, empathy without fragility, and conviction without arrogance.

The same uncertainty that defined wartime operations now defines everyday life. In business, in education, even in our families—sometimes *especially* in our families—people are looking for leaders who can hold composure when everything around them shakes.

I started reading research that confirmed what I was already seeing. Studies from multiple major universities all pointed to the same thing: trust is disappearing, leaders are burning out, and the ones who keep their people steady are the ones who can regulate themselves. They model it. Their people feel it.[1]

So, here's what I've come to understand. Leadership isn't about command anymore. It's about mastery over yourself. It's about being grounded enough to turn down the noise and listen. The leaders people trust right now? They're the ones who figured out that strength and compassion aren't opposites. They're allies.

What the World Needs from Leaders Today

Leadership used to be about having answers. Now it's about creating environments where people can think, figure things out, and grow together, even when the path isn't clear.

Gallup conducted a 2024 study that found that less than one in four employees trust their organization's leadership. At the same time, they expect more from their leaders, not less. They want moral clarity, not polished speeches. They're not asking to be impressed anymore. They're asking to be believed.[2]

---

[1] Center for Creative Leadership. *The Crisis of Confidence in Leadership.* Harvard Business Review. *Burnout Is About Your Workplace, Not Your People.* Edmondson, A. *Psychological Safety and the Fearless Organization.*

[2] Gallup. *State of the Global Workplace* 2024, Edelman. *2024 Edelman Trust Barometer*

That shift is both daunting and liberating. It means leadership can no longer rely on charisma, hierarchy, or fear. Those tools might still yield compliance, but never commitment. I've seen the difference between a leader who demanded obedience and one who inspired loyalty. Obedience gets the job done; loyalty makes the mission matter. The same principle applies everywhere—in business, education, or family life. When people believe their leader stands *for* something, not just *in* something, they give more of themselves.

Also, teams are people, and they do not need or want flawless heroes. (There's no such thing!) They need and want grounded human beings. Leaders who can admit mistakes without collapsing under them. Leaders who choose transparency over performance, service over spotlight, and purpose over power.

I've seen time and time again that the most effective leaders are not the ones who dominate meetings; they're the ones who create a sense of psychological safety so others can speak up. They ask questions rather than defend positions. They know that authority without empathy breeds silence, and silence, in any team, is the first sign of fear.

That's where the DIAL model came from. I kept noticing four things that showed up in leaders people trusted. They stayed disciplined in their focus. They were guided by integrity. They showed up authentically. And they never stopped learning. When those four were working together, everything else seemed to fall into place.

How Experience Shaped the DIAL Model

Most leadership frameworks don't come from a classroom or a stack of research papers. They come from living long enough to notice that the same patterns keep showing up. That's exactly how the DIAL model emerged. I didn't invent it in a workshop. It revealed itself across years of watching what worked, what didn't, and what actually held up under pressure.

In my first book, I talked about four leadership attributes that kept surfacing: *preparedness, resilience, grit, and compassion.* At the time, I didn't realize those qualities were connected to something deeper. However, over the years, I kept seeing the same behaviors underneath every strong leader and every strong team. The patterns were already there, but the words showed up later: *discipline, integrity, authenticity, and learning always.*

And these four aren't separate buckets. They feed and regulate each other. Discipline supports integrity. Integrity makes authenticity believable. Authenticity creates space for real learning. And learning keeps the whole system alive. They work together, not apart.

I started to see *discipline* differently once I realized it wasn't about punishment or perfection; it was about presence. Discipline is what grounds you. It's showing up prepared. It's doing what you said you'd do. It's holding yourself to the same standard you expect from others. And it's not the grind-culture version of discipline people *love* to romanticize. True discipline also means knowing when to rest, when to pull back, and when to protect what matters. It's the balance between drive and boundaries.

Integrity came even earlier for me on a Sunday morning with my father. We went to get a newspaper to read an article about our cross-country race the day before. I jumped out of the car and walked toward one of those old-fashioned newspaper vending machines, the kind where you drop in a quarter, pull the metal handle, and the door swings open so you can grab a copy of the paper—a *single* copy.

Except that morning, when I pulled the handle, I was so excited about the article that I paid for one paper but grabbed five.

I walked back and got back into the car. He looked at me, then asked, "How many of those did you pay for?"

"One," I replied sheepishly.

Then, he got out of the car, walked back to the machine, and dropped in four more quarters, one for each copy I hadn't paid for.

That was the moment integrity stopped being something adults just *talked* about and became something I saw lived out. And it taught me something simple but permanent: you can't lead people if you cut corners when no one's watching (or when they are).

Later in the military, the decisions got bigger and more complicated, and sometimes they weren't between right and wrong at all but just between two imperfect options. Integrity became choosing the option that aligned most closely with our values, even when it was uncomfortable or costly.

Authenticity took longer. Early on, I tried to *perform* confidence. ("Fake it 'til you make it," right?) I tried to look like the officer who had it all together, even when I didn't.

During an exercise in Panama, which was my first big leadership opportunity after BUD/S, I was nervous and overcompensating. One of my teammates, Danny Dietz, called me out: "Sir, this isn't you."

It stung. My pride flared up. But he was right. I was leading from fear, not authenticity. Months later in Afghanistan, I admitted that to him. Sadly, Danny died on the battlefield not long after that, driving the lesson even further into my mind. It taught me what pretending costs and what authenticity gives back.

Learning was the thread running through everything. The best leaders I served with were never finished products. They didn't act as if they'd arrived. They stayed curious. They asked questions. They listened not just with their ears, but with their awareness. They noticed when someone walked into a room looking defeated and quietly asked if they were okay. They learned from books and mentors but also, just as much from failure, from watching, and from conversations behind closed doors.

When I stepped back and connected all the dots, I saw the cycle clearly:

Discipline creates structure.

Integrity builds trust.

Authenticity builds connection.

Learning creates growth.

Miss one, and the others wobble. But when all four are present, they reinforce and regulate one another. Preparedness, resilience, grit, and compassion—the traits I once thought of as standalone—are strengthened by these deeper behaviors.

And that's how the DIAL model was born, not as a theory but as a reflection. A mirror held up to years of experience—my experience and those of the people I was privileged to serve with. What was left standing wasn't complicated. It was the essentials of leadership stripped down to their core.

Not an academic model. A lived one.

The Four Pillars in Relationships

When I first started naming these four pillars, I treated them like separate traits, almost like they were in their own boxes. But the more I worked with them, the more I realized they operate like muscles in the same body. You can lean on one for a while, maybe even overdevelop it, but eventually, the imbalance shows up somewhere else.

I'll go into this in much more detail later, but here's the TLDR (too long, didn't read) version: DIAL without one of the four.

Again, leaning too heavily on a single trait creates imbalances. You've probably seen this in leaders before. Someone who's incredibly disciplined but comes across as rigid, or someone who's authentic and open but can't follow through on anything. None of these qualities works well in isolation. Leadership is about how they interact.

Discipline gives you direction. It keeps you locked in when life gets noisy and helps you follow through when it would be easier not to. But discipline without integrity eventually turns into control or people-pleasing disguised as structure. Integrity is what keeps discipline honest. It reminds you why you're doing the work in the first place.

However, even integrity has limits if there's no authenticity behind it. I've seen leaders who said all the right things but led from a place of fear. They checked the boxes but never connected with their people. Authenticity is what turns values into behavior that others can feel. And when it's grounded in integrity, it doesn't look like oversharing or trying too hard; it just looks real.

Learning is the piece that keeps everything from getting stale. Without learning, discipline becomes stubbornness, integrity becomes self-righteousness, and authenticity becomes "this is just who I am," which is usually code for not wanting to grow. Learning keeps you flexible. It reminds you that leadership shifts with seasons, teams, and circumstances. It's not about reacting faster; it's about adapting smarter.

The way I picture the DIAL model is exactly like adjusting the scope on a weapon. You don't set it once and never touch it again. You make small adjustments based on the conditions, the environment, and the target.

Leadership works the same way. Some seasons require more discipline; others call for stronger integrity or deeper authenticity. And each adjustment teaches you something that helps you make the next shot with a little more precision.

That's why the DIAL model isn't a checklist. It's a rhythm. These four elements play off each other, creating a balance between structure and softness, conviction and curiosity, and clarity and compassion. When they're all working together, leadership feels less like something you're trying to perform and more like something you naturally embody.

When the Dial Slips

Even the best leaders sometimes lose their balance. The danger isn't in the slipping itself; it's in pretending you haven't. From what I've seen, leadership doesn't collapse overnight; it erodes one small compromise at a time.

I've lived through that drift. As I mentioned earlier about my experience in Panama, it was only Danny calling me out that brought me back to a place where I understood that I had drifted off course. I was no longer *dialed in.* I told myself I was protecting authority, but in truth, I was protecting ego. What I couldn't see then was that every layer of pretense builds distance. When you lead from behind a mask, your people stop seeing you, and worse, they stop believing *you* see *them.*

Recalibrating begins with awareness. For me, it meant asking hard questions:

Where am I over-rotating?
Where have I let ego replace integrity?
Where am I disconnected from my voice?

When the dial slips, we need to learn to slow down long enough to listen, not only to others but also to our internal compass. Each time I've paused to realign, the same truth surfaces: the dial is never broken; it just needs calibration. And calibration doesn't require a grand reset; it just requires a series of small, honest corrections.

Many people, including me, talk about resilience as bouncing back. But now, I've come to see it as more. Real resilience is *re-centering.* It's the discipline of returning to your values when fatigue, tragedy, or fear pulls you off course. The leaders who last aren't the ones who never falter; they're the ones who recognize the drift early and have the humility to correct it.

From Battlefield to Boardroom

People often assume that leadership in combat and leadership in corporate life couldn't be more different. The stakes, they say, are incomparable.

In my opinion, however, both are arenas of consequence. Both demand clarity and decisions that affect real people. Whether the mission is on foreign soil or in a conference room, the same human forces are at play: fear, ego, fatigue, loyalty, and the need to be seen and led.

When I left the Navy and began working with corporate teams, I expected to find a completely different environment. Instead, I saw familiar dynamics. Yes, there were no uniforms or ranks, but there were hierarchies just as rigid (sometimes more so). There were no physical battles, but the emotional terrain could be just as intense. I met executives who carried the same exhaustion I'd seen in deployed operators: men and women running at full speed, *performing* leadership rather than *embodying* it. They weren't lacking intelligence or drive. What they lacked was alignment—the same misalignment I'd felt years before in Panama, when I led from behind a mask, behind fear, and behind ego instead of from truth.

What I realized is that leadership stress doesn't always look like combat, but it is stress, nonetheless. Sometimes it looks like a founder trying to keep her company afloat, or a principal facing another underfunded school year, or a parent navigating a child's anxiety. The settings differ, but the emotional weight is heavy regardless: fear of failure, the burden of responsibility, and the isolation that comes with being the one everyone looks to when things fall apart.

That's why I say leadership isn't a profession. It's a way of life. And the same principles that sustain a team under fire are the ones that sustain a business team under strain.

I watched how the same principles showed up everywhere. Discipline? It became consistent. The ability to do what you said you'd do, even when no one's checking. Integrity became trust. Making decisions you could defend, even when they cost you something. Authenticity became connection. Letting people see that you're human, not some invincible figure. And learning became humility. The willingness to listen, to adapt, and to grow alongside your people instead of pretending you already have all the answers.

However, knowing these principles and living them are two completely different things. Anyone can nod along and say, "Yes, I should be more authentic" or "I need to stay grounded." The real work happens when pressure shows up. When you're tired, when stakes are high, when everything in you wants to react instead of respond—that's when it matters.

2

From the SEAL Teams to Teaching Mindfulness

Before I get any further into DIAL, I feel like I owe you some backstory. But the backstory also plays a major part later, so I'll give you the 30,000-foot view now and get deeper later.

In 2005, I was involved in an operation that went horribly sideways: Operation Red Wings in Afghanistan. We lost a lot of great guys, and I was sitting behind a desk when it all happened. That caused me a lot of moral injury and survivor's guilt because I wasn't out there on the battlefield physically helping them.

When I returned to the States, I struggled. I secretly addressed the pain and shame I was feeling by drinking and abusing prescription medication. After years, I found myself in a very dark place.

The restlessness became too heavy to ignore. I was impatient, distracted, and short-tempered. Sleep came in fragments, and my thoughts were slow. I could lead men through battle, but I couldn't sit through stillness.

Eventually, someone suggested I see a counselor. I remember sitting in this counselor's office, arms crossed, waiting for him to tell me something actionable. I expected a list of habits, plans, and strategies. Instead, he asked if I had ever tried mindfulness and meditation.

I remember laughing out loud because I found the idea so crazy. Meditation was something for monks on mountaintops, not SEALs trained for war.

He smiled, patient. "What if I told you there's a pill that could improve your performance physically and mentally, personally and professionally?"

As a Special Operator, you're always looking for an edge, whether that's over the enemy or over your best friend standing right next to you. I told him I'd take it.

He said, "Good. The pill is called mindfulness." Dang. He'd tricked me.

The next morning, I tried it. I sat down, closed my eyes, and tried to meditate for an hour because if I was going to meditate, by God, I was going to crush it!

Well, within seconds, I was fidgeting and frustrated. My mind ricocheted between grocery lists, memories, and the craziness of sitting still on purpose. When I told him about it the next week, he laughed.

"Dude, that's like showing up for a marathon without training. Start with two minutes."

Then he taught me a breathing exercise.

Inhale for four counts.

Hold for four.

Exhale for four.

Hold again for four.

Box breathing, he called it. (Funny enough, I'd learned something similar in the Teams. I'll come back to that later.)

At first, it felt mechanical, pointless even. But later, I was sitting in traffic when someone cut me off. That old surge of anger shot through me—the road rage, the reflex to chase, to correct, and to regain control (aka flip this dude "the bird"). Instead, I caught myself. I remembered the box.

Inhale four. Hold four. Exhale four. Hold four.

The reaction softened. I could feel the distance open between the event and my response. It wasn't dramatic, but it was undeniable. For the first time, I realized control didn't have to mean force.

That small moment became a turning point.

I began practicing every day, starting with a few minutes in the morning, sometimes before sleep, sometimes in the car before walking into a meeting. I didn't call it meditation; I called it resetting.

Over time, I was able to do longer breathing exercises and then even "real meditation." My sleep improved. My thoughts slowed. I still felt pressure, but it didn't own me.

What surprised me most was how it changed my awareness. I started noticing details I would have missed before, like a teammate's hesitation, my impatience before someone finished speaking, and the tone of a conversation shifting beneath the words. The same situational awareness that had kept me alive in combat was beginning to appear inwardly.

Mindfulness was not about emptying the mind. It was about noticing the mind—noticing the thoughts and emotions. It was not a retreat. It was reconnaissance and the ability to observe without interference.

For the first time since before Operation Red Wings, I felt a familiar sense of mastery.

Not over the mission, but over myself.

What Mindfulness Really Is

Enough with that backstory, let's talk more about mindfulness because it's foundational to DIAL.

Mindfulness is not softness. It is precision. It is the skill of being so aware of the present moment that you can meet it exactly as it is—not as you fear it, or hope it, or wish it to be.

When I began teaching this work, I often used a simple comparison. In combat, situational awareness is everything. You learn to notice what others miss.

Mindfulness is the same discipline turned inward. It's internal situational awareness, which ironically improves your external situational awareness. You begin to track your own terrain: your thoughts, emotions, impulses, and the tightening of your jaw before a reaction.

The benefit isn't control in the traditional sense; it's clarity. You start to see your mind the way you'd study a map: identifying obstacles, routes, and blind spots.

I started looking into the research to understand what was happening in the brain. Scientists at the University of Zurich and other institutions found something interesting. When leaders practice mindfulness, three things are strengthened: attention, awareness, and authenticity.[3]

Attention is staying locked on what matters when everything is pulling you in different directions. Awareness is sensing what's happening in a moment before you react to it. And authenticity is having the courage to align your behavior with your values, even when it costs you. When you have all three working, that's when presence happens. That's when people feel like you're there with them, not just physically present but mentally and emotionally present.

Presence isn't stillness of body; it's simply attention. It's the opposite of distraction. It is the ability to be fully present where you are, even in motion.

In a 2019 study published in *Frontiers in Psychology*, mindful leaders were consistently rated by their teams as more trustworthy and more effective, not because of charisma but because of how they showed up. Mindfulness strengthens the brain systems responsible for empathy and emotional regulation, which allows leaders to stay composed enough to truly listen, and listening, when done fully, is one of the rarest forms of respect.[4]

---

[3]   Borge Doornich & Helen Miller Lynch (2024). The mindful leader: a review of leadership qualities derived from mindfulness meditation.

[4]   Arendt, J. F. W., Kolste, M., & Nielsen, R. (2019). Mindfulness and leadership: Communication as a mechanism linking leaders' dispositional mindfulness with followers' satisfaction. Frontiers in Psychology, 10, 667. https://doi.org/10.3389/fpsyg.2019.00667

When I began coaching, I thought my job was to find solutions quickly, to offer strategies and frameworks. However, the more I practiced mindfulness, the more I realized that real progress came from listening differently and noticing not just what someone said, but how they said it. That kind of awareness doesn't come from analysis. It comes from presence.

Mindfulness creates the presence you need. It gives you the inner stability to shift between the four traits, to move fluidly, to DIAL in on what each moment demands. It keeps perception clean and allows emotion to inform your judgment without hijacking it, or at least to notice when it has been hijacked. It widens the gap between what happens and how you respond, the space in which leaders operate.

When I speak about mindfulness now, I don't speak of it as a practice. I speak of it as the foundational lifestyle upon which the DIAL model works.

You can't navigate these four dimensions unless you're grounded first. And mindfulness is how you get there. It's not the only way, but it's the fastest way I know.

Why It Works

For a long time, I thought composure was a personality trait. Some people stayed cool; others didn't. Years later, I learned it's not completely biological. It's a trainable state, not a fixed one.

Every human being carries a built-in alarm system designed to protect them. When a threat appears, the amygdala fires, adrenaline surges, and cortisol floods the bloodstream. Your vision narrows. Your body prepares for movement. In combat, that reaction saves lives, but when it becomes constant, and your body keeps firing even without danger, it turns from an asset into a liability.

That's what happens to most leaders today. They live as though the proverbial battlefield never ends. Though to a lesser extent, emails, deadlines, and important decisions can trigger the same chemical flood as a firefight. Our bodies perceive all these, along with many other stimuli, as threats.

When you slow your breathing and pay deliberate attention, your nervous system shifts gears. The parasympathetic branch, responsible for rest and recovery, activates. The body receives a simple but profound message and relays it onward to the brain: you are safe.

Scientists at Harvard and Massachusetts General Hospital found that when you practice mindfulness regularly, your brain literally changes. Your prefrontal cortex—the part that handles judgment, empathy, and emotional control—gets stronger and more active. At the same time, your amygdala—the fear center— quiets down. The result? Less emotional volatility. Better executive control. Your brain actually rewires.[5]

Even modest mindfulness practices can create real, measurable change.

Here's what surprised me about the research: you don't need hours of meditation to see measurable change. Thirteen minutes a day for eight weeks, and you start sharpening your attention, strengthening your working memory. Some studies showed gains in focus and reduced mind wandering in just two weeks. For leaders dealing with constant input, that's huge. That means steadier decision-making, clearer thinking under pressure, and fewer reactive, heat-of-the-moment choices.

One of the simplest ways to access these benefits is through the breath. Techniques like the box breathing I mentioned earlier can engage your vagus nerve, the main communication line between your brain, heart, lungs, and gut.

Slow, deliberate breathing shifts your body toward calm, steadies your heart rate, softens your stress response, and restores your physiological coherence. From that state, the prefrontal cortex

---

[5]   Lazar, S. W., et al. (2011). Mindfulness meditation practice leads to increases in regional brain gray matter concentration. Psychiatry Research: Neuroimaging, 191(1), 36–43.

switches back on, giving you better emotional control, sharper judgment, and the ability to respond rather than react.

I want to be very clear here. Mindfulness doesn't remove stress; it changes your relationship to it. Instead of fighting it, you learn to ride it, using awareness as the stabilizer.

Another great thing about mindfulness (do you really need another?) is that it enhances metacognition, which is the awareness of awareness. It gives you the ability to step back and observe your thoughts before they turn into actions.

The practical value of that skill is enormous. It means you can notice a flash of anger before it becomes a reaction. In leadership, milliseconds matter. The space between reaction and response is where trust is built or broken. Mindfulness widens that space and lets you think while others are still tightening their grip.

I've seen this transformation repeatedly in executives, athletes, service members, and parents (myself absolutely included). Once they learn to regulate their physiology, their leadership changes tone because mindfulness trains the nervous system for leadership. It teaches you how to hold composure when conditions don't. It rewires the reflexes that once equated speed with strength, replacing them with discernment.

Stillness, I've learned, doesn't dull perception. It refines it. It's the difference between reacting to every sound in the dark and learning to distinguish which sounds matter.

The Power of Presence

We had a saying in the Special Operations community: slow is smooth, and smooth is fast. It sounds like a contradiction, but it describes something essential about performance. When you slow down enough to be deliberate, your movements become precise. Precision becomes rhythm, and rhythm becomes speed. By precision, I mean removing every unnecessary motion, anxious impulse, and every reaction born of fear.

That same principle applies to leadership. The more reactive you are, the more errors you make. The calmer you are, the clearer the signal you send.

Mindfulness is what creates that calm. It is not detachment. It is a deliberate groundedness that allows you to move through chaos without magnifying it.

As I mentioned before, when I began working with senior leaders in the corporate world, I noticed something familiar. Their worlds were different from the battlefield, but their symptoms were the same: overextension, tunnel vision, decision fatigue, and exhaustion disguised as drive. They were brilliant, but they were burning from the inside out. They weren't leading their companies. Their nervous systems were.

Mindfulness offered them what it had given me: space. For leaders, this space makes room for precision.

Space to notice before acting.

Space to hear before speaking.

Space to lead without losing yourself in the noise.

In that space, precision returns. You begin to sense when to speak and when to wait, when to press and when to pause. You start reading the room differently. You're scanning for subtle shifts, anticipating movement before it happens.

You gain the ability to move through complexity without drawing unnecessary attention or creating unnecessary disturbance, and others feel that. They feel that sense of safety even in the face of uncertainty. They trust those who can absorb volatility without passing it along. That is the practical side of mindfulness. It's not necessarily serenity, but stability.

The longer I practiced, the more I saw how this peace of mind underpinned every part of the DIAL framework.

Discipline begins with awareness. You can't sustain what you don't notice. The leader who disciplines attention can discipline action.

Integrity depends on presence. You can only align your actions with your values if you are aware of the pull to deviate.

Authenticity emerges from stillness. When you stop performing for approval, all that remains is who you really are.

Learning requires humility, and humility is the willingness to observe your mistakes without judgment. Mindfulness gives you that perspective.

As with these pillars, each relies on the others; without mindfulness, they fall apart. Discipline turns into rigidity. Integrity becomes image management. Authenticity slips into oversharing. Learning becomes accumulation instead of growth.

Mindfulness—presence—holds them together.

It's easy to underestimate how much a leader's inner state shapes a team's outer performance. The truth is that emotion is contagious. Anxiety spreads faster than instruction. A single unregulated reaction from a leader can shift the entire mood of a room or of a team. But calm is contagious, too. When people sense stability, they begin to steady themselves. When they sense awareness, they start to reflect.

The Box Breathing Drill

The first breathing exercise I ever learned came from the SEAL Teams, and I had it reintroduced to me by that counselor I mentioned before. He called it box breathing: four counts in, four counts hold, four counts out, four counts hold. Do this four times. We'd done something like this in the Teams on the shooting range, but we called it tactical breathing. Of course, with a cool name like that, I didn't have any problem doing it.

It slowed our heart rate and respiratory rate so we could shoot better. But I'd never thought to use it in everyday life when I got stressed out. It sounded almost trivial. I remember thinking that if breathing were really the answer, every person I knew would already be enlightened.

Going back to the afternoon when I was sitting in traffic, and someone cut me off. It was an ordinary moment, but my body reacted as if it were a threat. My pulse spiked, jaw tightened, and the same reflex that once prepared me for combat now surged in the middle of a freeway.

But I caught myself. I remembered the technique.

Inhale four. Hold four. Exhale four. Hold four. Do this four times.

Something shifted—not dramatically, but enough. The reaction softened. Space appeared between what happened and what I felt about it. That small space—the pause—was everything. It gave me room to choose.

That's what mindfulness really trains: the capacity to insert choice into places that used to be automatic.

The practice is simple.

Inhale through your nose for a slow count of four.

Hold for four.

Exhale through your mouth for four.

Hold again for four.

Repeat three to five times.

That's all. No candles, no chants, no special posture. Just awareness.

The power lies in what happens underneath the surface. When you breathe this way, the vagus nerve signals the body that it is safe, and the body relays that message to the brain. Heart rate drops. Blood pressure steadies. The brain re-engages its reasoning centers instead of running survival scripts. The body, brain, and nervous systems all move from reaction to regulation and response.

Over time, those small acts of regulation compound. You begin to notice stress earlier and release it faster. You start recognizing the signals—the shallow breath, the clenched shoulders, the tightening jaw—and can intervene before tension becomes temper.

I practiced box breathing before mission briefs, during flights, and in the moments before sleep. Later, I used it backstage before keynotes and between coaching calls. It became a reset button. It was (is) a way to ground the mind, no matter where I was (am).

Leaders tell me all the time that they "don't have time" for mindfulness. I get that instinct as the pace feels relentless. One of the best replies I've heard to that was from a Special Forces guy we had on our podcast (*Men Talking Mindfulness*). He said, "That's like saying you're too dirty to shower."

The reality is that something like box breathing takes less than two minutes. You can do it before you walk into a meeting, after a hard conversation, or while sitting in your car before heading home. The setting doesn't matter. What matters is paying attention. You're just giving yourself a moment to reset.

Think of it as training the body to obey composure. Over time, that composure becomes reflex.

When practiced consistently, this single technique rewires the relationship between stress and performance. The nervous system learns that calm doesn't mean weakness. It means control. And control doesn't come from suppression; it comes from attention.

I've seen this shift transform how people lead. When someone learns to regulate their state, they stop reacting to every stress signal around them. They start influencing tone instead of absorbing it. They enter meetings differently. The energy in the room changes. They listen longer. They respond later. And their teams begin to mirror that.

Box breathing, at its simplest, is leadership in microform. It's the act of creating space before response.

That's what the battlefield had taught me to do with my surroundings. Mindfulness taught me to do it within myself.

Stillness begins with a single breath—not the dramatic kind we take after a crisis, but the slow, deliberate kind we choose before it begins.

Before discipline can be applied, the nervous system has to be steady. Before integrity can guide a decision, the mind has to be clear enough to hear it. Before authenticity can connect, the leader has to be present. And before learning can happen, there has to be enough space to notice what's really going on.

Mindfulness doesn't replace leadership skills. It makes them accessible under pressure.

Once you can regulate your internal state, you can begin to act with intention rather than reaction. You can keep promises to yourself. You can show up consistently. You can do the work that matters, even when it's uncomfortable or unseen.

That's where discipline enters.

3

Discipline

In 2019, Eliud Kipchoge became the first person in history to run a marathon in under two hours. (For context, that's 4:34 per mile for 26.2 miles. My fastest *single* mile ever was 4:37, and I thought that was pretty good!) The world saw the final stretch: the cameras, the pacers, and the crowds lining the course. What almost no one saw were the years of discipline that made that moment possible.

Kipchoge trains in a small camp in Kenya where the days look almost identical. Wake up early. Sweep the floors of the training compound. Run. Eat simply. Rest. Repeat.

No spotlight. No social media fanfare. No shortcuts. When asked why he lives this way, he responded, "Only the disciplined ones are free." (Similar to my fellow retired Navy SEAL, Jocko Willink's line, "Discipline equals freedom.")

What he meant was simple: discipline isn't about pushing harder. It's about removing the things that pull you off course. It's doing the right work long after motivation fades. It's the reps nobody sees, and no one celebrates, and it's the choices that build a sense of trust in yourself.

The idea that discipline is built in the unseen moments is something I've learned repeatedly. When I look back over my life from running cross country in Ruston to serving as a Navy SEAL to being a dad, one lesson shows up everywhere: discipline changes everything.

My high school coach was the first one to really drill that into me. He wasn't loud or dramatic, and he wasn't trying to motivate us with some big locker-room speech. He just expected effort. Every week, he'd write our training plan on the board and say, "See the board. Stick to the plan." No fanfare. No babysitting. And he didn't need to check up on us as the results told the truth.

Discipline isn't about being forced to do something; it's about becoming someone. Those miles we ran before sunrise, during lunch break, or after sunset built a lot more than endurance. They built trust—first with myself and then with the guys next to me. It's a form of honesty you can see: doing what you said you'd do, especially when no one is watching.

In my first platoon, we had a platoon chief who never raised his voice and never tried to intimidate anyone, but he was very disciplined. He showed up early, knew his gear better than anyone, and lived the exact standard he expected from us. Because he lived it, we followed it. He showed us that discipline isn't something you teach; it's something you show.

And that's really the heart of discipline: doing what you said you'd do long after the feeling that made you say it, often short-lived motivation, has faded. It's the gap between potential and proof.

The Strength Behind Every Great Team

The teams that truly perform at a high level are made up of folks who show up the same way on easy days and hard ones. That quiet reliability is what makes a team feel grounded.

Discipline is what creates that reliability. It's the backbone of trust. In the Teams, we had tons of flaws just like any other group, but most of the time, you knew the guy next to you had done what he needed to do. That kind of reliability helped us stay focused on the mission rather than waste time on doubt.

You see the same pattern in business, in families, in sports, and anywhere people have to rely on each other. Everyone knows Michael Jordan for his talent and fire, but the Bulls wouldn't have become a dynasty without Scottie Pippen. He didn't chase headlines. He didn't need a hype reel. He just showed up every game, did the work most people never noticed, and delivered the same standard night after night. That quiet reliability lifted the whole team. That's discipline. It's the steady hands that make everyone else steadier.

Then there was Kobe Bryant. He showed the same principle, just through a different lens. People talk about his intensity, but what truly sets him apart is his consistency. (I'll talk more about consistency here in just a bit.) His teammates would show up for an early session and find him already deep into a workout, but that wasn't a stunt. It wasn't for show. That was simply his everyday rhythm. He trained the same way he played—with predictable, repeatable habits. His discipline wasn't about being extreme; it was about removing doubt. He prepared so thoroughly that when pressure hit, he didn't have to "rise to the occasion." He just did what he always did. Kobe's steadiness raised the bar. Pippen's steadiness anchored the team.

Different expressions, same truth: discipline lifts the whole group, whether it's loud or silent, visible or behind the scenes. It's the consistency, not the theatrics, that changes outcomes.

Disciplined leadership doesn't just make individual people better; it changes the environment they work in. When a leader is clear, prepared, and steady under pressure, the whole team settles. People stop managing personalities and start solving problems. Meetings get shorter. Communication gets cleaner. Conflicts get simpler. Decision-making speeds up because everyone understands the standard.

That's the real effect of discipline: it removes unnecessary friction so the real work can happen.

And here's the part a lot of folks miss: discipline isn't about tightening your grip. It's about giving people something stable enough so they can take risks, speak up, and perform without fear that the ground will shift beneath them.

A disciplined leader doesn't just bring predictability to chaos. They create the conditions where others can excel. That's when you stop leading through pressure and start leading through trust.

What Discipline Really Means

Most people think discipline is about grinding harder, but real discipline is quieter than that. It's the moment after the motivation fades, when no one is watching, when you're tired, when you feel pulled in five different directions, and you still do the thing you said you'd do. That's the moment where you either build trust with yourself or chip away at it.

I tell my clients this all the time: discipline isn't built in grand gestures. It's built on small agreements that are kept repeatedly. Those everyday choices: the workout, the honest conversation, the five minutes of meditation. Sticking to these small agreements is what shapes who you become as a leader—not because they're impressive, but because they're consistent.

And the interesting part? Your brain responds to those choices. It adapts. Every time you follow through on something difficult, you strengthen the circuitry responsible for effort and emotional regulation. In other words, you train yourself to stay steady under stress. That's why disciplined people look calm in chaos. Their brains have had more reps staying on course.

Motivation may start the process, but it can't carry it.

Discipline is what takes over when the excitement wears off.

It's the bridge between the person you want to be and the person you show up as.

The Neuroscience of Doing Hard Things

I mentioned the science behind all this a second ago. Let's dig into that a little more here. (As I write that, all I can think of is Will Ferrell as Ron Burgundy in *Anchorman*: "It's science!")

For most of my life, I understood this truth through experience: do hard things consistently, and over time, they stop feeling so hard. But later, I realized the neuroscience lines up perfectly.

I started listening to a neuroscientist named Andrew Huberman, who runs a podcast where he breaks down how the brain works. He talks about motivation, stress, focus, and behavior change, stuff that matters. And one of the things he keeps coming back to is how discipline gets built in the brain.

There's a part of your brain called the anterior mid-cingulate cortex—basically the region that decides whether you lean in or back off when something gets hard. Every time you follow through on something difficult, you strengthen that region. Your brain literally rewires itself. You're training it to stay calm and take action the next time you face discomfort.

That means every act of discipline compounds: finishing the workout you didn't want to start, following through on a promise when skipping would be easier, and sitting in meditation when your mind is fighting you. Those aren't just habits. They're reps for your brain. Huberman calls this "training the effort system." The more you use it, the stronger it gets.

But—and this is *big*—it works the other way, too.

If doing hard things strengthens that system, avoiding them weakens it. Skip enough workouts, avoid hard conversations, hit snooze instead of getting up, and your brain starts adapting to that pattern instead. It learns that discomfort should be avoided, and over time, you start believing you can't do hard things. That identity settles in fast—super fast. (It happens faster this way than the opposite.)

And once you see yourself that way, your actions follow.

That's why consistency matters more than intensity. One small hard thing every day is far more powerful than one huge push occasionally. You're not trying to impress anyone. You're teaching your brain to trust yourself.

Discipline—It's Not About Intensity

Discipline isn't about effort levels. It's about repeatability. And one of the clearest examples of that came from a story most of us know.

When US Airways Flight 1549 went through a flock of birds and lost both engines over the Hudson River, Captain Chesley "Sully" Sullenberger had seconds—seconds—to make decisions that would save or cost lives. There was no checklist for what he faced, no time for emotion, and no margin for error.

Yet every report from that cockpit said the same thing: he was calm, direct, and steady. (I get goose bumps every time I think about this.)

That wasn't adrenaline. That wasn't a heroic surge. That was decades of disciplined preparation doing exactly what disciplined preparation is supposed to do.

Just like Kobe, Sully didn't rise to the occasion. He fell back on the standard he had lived for years.

And 155 people walked off that plane because of it.

That's the real nature of discipline, not louder, not harder, not more, but steadier.

People don't trust leaders because they're charismatic. They trust them because they're consistent.

And that consistency matters even more when the world gets unpredictable. In the field, you can't control the weather, the terrain, the timeline, or the hundred variables waiting to go sideways. But you can control how you prepare and how you show up. That's where discipline becomes real.

The same thing shows up in business and family life. When the leader is steady, the group can focus. When the leader wobbles, uncertainty spreads fast. If you preach punctuality but show up late, people notice. If you demand accountability but let things slide, the gap is obvious.

Discipline builds trust. Inconsistency breaks it—every time.

And discipline isn't only about pushing forward. It's also about pulling back when that's the wiser move. There's discipline in rest, in recovery, and in reflection. There's discipline in saying no when yes would burn you out. I've watched leaders brag about never stopping as if exhaustion is a leadership trait. It's not.

Real discipline has a rhythm: effort and recovery, action and pause, drive and restraint.

Sometimes the hardest discipline is stepping back, delegating, or trusting your team to carry the load. But disciplined leaders don't prove their worth through exhaustion. They prove it by being someone their people can count on day after day.

That steadiness is the foundation for everything else in the DIAL model.

Building Discipline Through Practice

When I talk to clients about discipline, everyone nods. They want to be more consistent, more grounded, and more balanced.

Then we start small: journaling, a daily walk, ten minutes of meditation. Two weeks later, I check in, and half the time, I hear, "I haven't started."

That's the real work because discipline isn't about knowing what to do. It's about doing it, especially when it's inconvenient or uncomfortable. The clients who follow through, even on the smallest actions, are the ones who grow the fastest.

I've watched people gain confidence, communicate better, feel calmer, and change their health not because of one big leap, but because they made small, hard choices every day: a short walk, a journal entry, a pause before reacting. Those choices compound. They make people better leaders.

For most of us, discipline starts with the basics:

- Journaling for self-awareness

- Exercise for physical and mental strength

- Meditation for calm and focus

- Eating well to fuel the day
- Sleep to think clearly

Even something as simple as waking up just twenty minutes earlier or backward-planning your morning builds discipline. Most people move through life reactively; discipline creates intention.

It's not about perfection or punishment. It's the alignment between what you say matters and what you do. And the more you keep those small promises to yourself, the easier it becomes to keep them with others: your team, your family, and your goals.

Discipline spreads. In every high-performing team I've ever seen, accountability was shared. I'm sure you've seen the same things in high-performing teams you were a part of. You could trust the person next to you to hold the line. Their standards raised yours, and yours raised theirs. But discipline alone doesn't guarantee you're holding the right line.

You can build disciplined habits, tight systems, and consistent execution, and still drift if those behaviors aren't anchored to something deeper. Discipline tells you how to act. It doesn't tell you why.

That's where integrity enters.

Integrity is what gives discipline direction. It's the internal compass that determines which standards matter, which shortcuts are unacceptable, and which lines don't move, even when no one is watching.

Without integrity, discipline becomes mechanical.

With it, discipline becomes meaningful.

4

Integrity

Years ago, in the early days of Patagonia, founder Yvon Chouinard walked into one of his production facilities unannounced. He wasn't there to give a speech or check numbers. He just wanted to see how people worked.

After a few minutes of watching the line, he noticed something small but telling: perfectly good scraps of material being wasted. Stuff that could easily be reused was getting tossed into the trash—not because anyone was lazy or trying to cut corners, just because it was faster and nobody was paying attention.

Most leaders would've shrugged it off. Nobody outside the building would ever know. The product would still ship. The customers would still buy it.

But Chouinard stopped the whole line.

He walked over, picked up a handful of those scraps from the trash, and then said this: "If we're going to say we care about the world, then we don't get to cut corners when the world isn't watching."

He didn't do this for publicity; instead of lecturing his team, he worked beside them for the rest of the day, reorganizing the space so that doing the right thing became the norm, not the exception.

That's integrity—just a small moment when a leader's private behavior matched his public values.

Integrity is one of those words people use often but, clearly, don't always live. It sounds clear until the moment it's tested. When loyalty collides with conscience, when doing what's right means standing alone, *that* is when integrity stops being a *principle* and becomes a *practice*.

The Weight of a Decision

Every military operation begins with a plan: maps spread out across tables, different units planning different stages of the op, a dozen moving parts trying to synchronize. In Afghanistan in June 2005, Operation Red Wings began like all the others, but somewhere deep down, I felt something was off.

It wasn't about fear or readiness. I don't know. Maybe it was. There was an unease that wouldn't go away. The terrain was unforgiving. The timing was rushed. There were too many units, unfamiliar with each other, and we didn't have all the assets that normally supported a mission of this risk. The gap between what we had and what we needed was enough to make my stomach tighten. I didn't think we were ready. I didn't *feel* we were ready.

I spoke up. "Gents, I know I'm a brand-new guy, but I feel that we need more time. We need more intel." My words landed softly and disappeared into the hum of authority.

Others disagreed.

"We're good to go," I was told. "We've done more with less."

I wanted to believe that. I wanted to trust that the experience of those above me outweighed the feeling rising in my chest. But something in me knew the risk was different this time. At that moment, I faced a kind of test that doesn't appear in any guidebook or field manual: the test of integrity under pressure. I remember standing there, trying to decide whether to push harder, to be the one who disrupted momentum for the sake of safety. Instead, I folded. I told myself I had done my part by raising the concern and trusted the chain of command.

I've thought about that choice for years. I replayed it long after the operation ended in tragedy. I can't say my voice alone would have changed the outcome. But what I know for certain is that I stopped short of doing everything I could. And that's the part that still stays with me.

At the Naval Academy, we were taught a simple definition of integrity: *doing the right thing, even when no one is looking.* But the longer I served, the more I learned that the *real* test of integrity isn't just when no one's watching; it can come when everyone *is watching,* and you're the only one who disagrees.

That day, I learned that silence can feel safe, but it leaves a mark. I felt like a coward.

Integrity isn't about being right; it's about being *real.* It's about listening to that inner compass that tells you when something is off, even if you can't justify it with data or hierarchy.

Looking back, I can still feel the weight of that decision. Integrity, I've learned, doesn't shout. It whispers. It warns. It gives you that sinking feeling in your gut that something isn't aligned. The question is whether you listen before the cost becomes irreversible.

When Integrity Demands Courage

When I look back on that mission, the memory that always surfaces first isn't the firefight or the chaos that followed. It's a short, human conversation.

We were going to send four men into the hills on a reconnaissance mission to gather intelligence before a follow-on assault mission: Michael "Murph" Murphy, Marcus Luttrell, Matt Axelson, and Danny Dietz. The night before, Danny pulled me aside. He called me "Mac," as everyone did. His voice carried something I hadn't heard from him before: fear.

"Hey, Mr. Mac," he said, "I'm scared."

Danny wasn't the type to show fear. He was steady, reliable, the kind of man who could find peace or even create peace anywhere. For him to admit that, even in a whisper, told me everything I needed to know. His intuition matched mine: something—or *somethings*—about this mission was off.

I remember the way the air felt that night, and how that same knot in my stomach tightened. Everything in me wanted to believe it would go as planned. I had already raised my concerns in the planning room, but I hadn't pressed hard enough. When the decision was made to move forward, I went along with it. The guys had rehearsed; they'd prepared. Still, I couldn't stop the unease. Something fundamental had been ignored.

That's another part of leadership no one prepares you for: the weight of knowing you were right but not loud enough.

Almost immediately after the operation began, the first signs that something was wrong appeared: a fast rope cut away rather than pulled back into the helicopter, a broken transmission, and a missed check-in. Then the team was compromised by goat herders. In that terrain, in that conflict, it didn't take much imagination to know what would come next.

Releasing the herders was the right thing to do morally, legally, and tactically. But everyone understood the reality: word travels fast in the mountains. The enemy doesn't wait. Before long, a report came in: troops in contact, a "TIC." Our boys were in a firefight.

When that word hits an operations center, a hundred decisions that used to have space suddenly compress into seconds. Everyone moves at once, ideally with discipline, not panic. The urgency is real.

We immediately spun up the Quick Reaction Force (QRF): multiple helicopters, multiple crews, everyone moving with intensity. They were moving with the kind of purpose that comes from knowing teammates' lives depend on the speed and clarity of your next decisions.

Once the QRF lifted off, the operations center grew still. No one sat. No one relaxed. We all just kind of hovered between hope and dread. You listen to the rhythms of the radio, the cadence of each voice, the space between transmissions. Those spaces tell you as much as the words do.

Then the call came that still lives in my memories, my dreams, and my heart (and I fully acknowledge this isn't exclusively my burden to bear).

One of the helicopters—an MH-47 loaded with sixteen men, eight Navy SEALs and eight Army Night Stalkers—had been hit by an RPG.

It had gone down.

It's strange how quiet a room can get when something that devastating hits. You expect shouting, scrambling, something. But what you get is a silence so heavy that breathing feels like a violation. Some stare at the floor. Some stare straight ahead. Some stare at nothing at all. There were no survivors from the helicopter, and now the fate of the guys on the ground was completely unknown.

There is no way to write this without the weight showing up on the page, no framing that makes it lighter, and no lesson that redeems it. Leadership in moments like this is about staying present when people are looking to you for steadiness that you don't fully feel yourself.

I wasn't in the air that day, and I wasn't on that mountainside. I was behind a screen in Bagram watching updates refresh in jagged fragments. In some ways, that made it harder. SEALs aren't wired to sit still in moments like that. We're wired to move, to go toward the danger, and to put our hands on the problem. But that day, I couldn't go anywhere. I could only witness.

In the days that followed, before we knew the fate of the guys on the ground, my junior guys kept glancing at me, not for direction, but for calibration. How do we act? How do we carry this? How do we keep functioning when the worst-case scenario just punched a hole through our chests?

I pulled them aside, not into formation but into a small circle—a human circle. We talked about the brothers we lost and those we feared were lost, about the things they loved, and the stories we had lived with them. We didn't try to analyze tactics or piece together a timeline. We laughed. We cried. We yelled. We tried to keep our humanity intact.

The Aftermath

Days later, the remains of the sixteen men from the downed MH-47 were brought back to Bagram. The ramp ceremony that followed was unlike anything I'd ever experienced.

Flag-draped caskets. Total silence, except for the bagpipes and the wind. Rows of uniforms standing at attention, their faces hard but their eyes full of pain—many filled with tears.

Nobody gave a speech. The moment itself did the talking.

We loaded the caskets onto a C-17 cargo plane in formation, saluting each. It was grief with structure. It was a ritual holding back collapse—at least partially.

Recovering Murph and Dietz

Not long after the initial ceremony, Air Force PJs recovered two bodies from the field: Michael Murphy ("Murph") and Danny.

By that time, the lone survivor of the operation, Marcus Luttrell, had been recovered. Matt Axelson was still unaccounted for, though all of us felt the truth closing in.

Murph and Danny were brought back to Bagram in body bags, each draped with a flag. I was part of a small group that helped identify them. There is no training that makes that task easier. There is no version of "being ready" for it. It's a moment that strips away everything except duty, respect, and an ache that has no language.

You do it because it must be done. You do it because they would've done it for you. You do it because integrity doesn't disappear when the job becomes unbearable.

We held a separate ramp ceremony for Murph and Danny, smaller but just as heavy. Their absence was a hole in the center of every man standing there.

Escorting Them Home

I was assigned, along with Matt Leathers, who unfortunately died years later in a free diving accident, to escort their remains home. Standing on the flight line as their caskets were prepared for transport, I remember the night air feeling impossibly still. The kind of stillness that makes you aware of every breath you take.

Before deployment, I'd asked the men on my team to write letters to their loved ones, the kind you hope will never be needed. Just a simple, sober act of preparation, making sure that, if the worst ever happened, there would be words waiting for the people who mattered most.

Danny wrote one for his wife, Patsy. I carried that letter with me.

When we landed stateside, I was exhausted in a way that had nothing to do with sleep. I hadn't seen my then-wife in months, and every part of me wanted to go home, even for a few minutes, to step into something familiar, something normal.

But Patsy was waiting, too.

She already knew the official story. She already had the facts. But facts don't fill the space left behind. She needed someone who had served beside Danny over "there."

And I had Danny's letter.

So instead of going home first, I went straight to her. I carried the folded flag that had draped his body bag and the letter he had typed with a steady hand long before any of us knew what was coming.

When I walked into her house, there were lots of friends there. Then I saw her. There's no script for that moment, no right opening line. I didn't try to offer comfort. That would have sounded hollow. I just handed her the flag, then the letter, and let the silence breathe for a moment.

She held the envelope the way people hold fragile things, as if it contained the last piece of him, which, in a way, it did. And then she talked, not about the war, not about the circumstances, but about Danny as a husband, as a friend, as the man she loved. I didn't try to fix her grief or soften it. I just listened.

I didn't go to her house to be noble, and I don't tell this story to paint myself that way. I went because it was the right thing to do. Leadership means being accountable for your people before, during, and after the mission.

That entire experience from the firefight, the QRF, the downed helicopter, the identification, the ceremonies, the escort home, the conversation with Patsy—reshaped my understanding of leadership. People don't follow you because you're fearless. They follow you because you're faithful.

Integrity Beyond the Battlefield

Losing people strips away the slogans and leaves you with what holds up. After coming home, I realized integrity doesn't show up only in dramatic moments. Most of the time, it lives in quiet decisions nobody notices.

It starts small: keeping your word, admitting mistakes early, telling the truth even when it slows things down. Those habits build muscle long before any high-stakes moment. The battlefield doesn't *create* integrity; it *reveals* it.

My dad taught me that long before the military. He never preached about integrity; he just lived it: returning extra change, helping without being asked, and doing the right thing quietly. Watching him taught me that integrity is about reliability, not attention.

Years later, when I had to own a bad call or take responsibility for someone else's mistake, his example was in the back of my mind. Integrity is a daily practice. Stop practicing, and it weakens.

On every team I've led, people pick up fast on whether their leader's standards stay steady. You can't fake consistency. People don't need perfection; they need to know they won't get a different version of you depending on the audience.

The real danger comes when it's easy to cut corners. Small compromises add up. A missed promise here, a bent rule there, and trust starts to crack.

True integrity isn't loud. It shows up in how you handle what isn't yours, how you talk about someone who isn't present, and how you treat people who can't give you anything in return. Those moments build credibility long before any crisis tests it.

I've come to see integrity as a quiet discipline: simple, steady, and easy to overlook. Training keeps your body ready; truth keeps your *character* ready. You don't get to choose all your challenges, but you choose the person you bring into them.

The Cost and Reward of Integrity

Integrity always sounds straightforward until you're tested. It's easy to talk about values when they fit the moment. It's a lot harder when they don't.

There are times when doing the right thing feels isolating, when you question a direction everyone else seems comfortable with, or when you refuse to ignore something that doesn't sit right. Those choices don't always earn applause. Sometimes they earn silence or distance. I've felt that. The looks that say, "Just let it go," the shift in the room after you speak up. It's uncomfortable.

Those moments make you wonder if it's worth it. But leadership built on convenience doesn't hold. Leadership built on *conviction* does. Integrity won't spare you from hard situations, but it keeps you from losing yourself inside them.

I've watched this play out repeatedly. Leaders who cut corners often rise quickly, but they rarely stay there. The ones who stay consistent even when it costs them build reputations that outlast any title. People trust leaders they can predict, not leaders who adjust their values depending on the situation.

Integrity also has a long memory. The same people who questioned your decision in the moment often come back later and admit they respected it. Time makes the picture clearer. The tough calls are usually the ones that define you. Credibility builds slowly and disappears quickly. Once trust breaks, you don't fix it with a speech; you rebuild it through steady behavior.

Integrity takes courage in the moment, but the reward is real: you don't have to wonder who you were in the tough spots. Your actions match your reflection. You sleep better. You stand a little taller. You stop explaining yourself because your behavior already did the explaining.

Integrity doesn't make leadership easier; it actually makes it much harder, but it also makes it solid. And that lasts long after recognition fades.

The Compass Within

We all have an internal compass—a compass that steadies you when things tilt off center, an alignment between what you believe and how you behave. You don't have to be flawless. You just have to keep correcting your course. That's how leaders earn trust and how they find their way back when everything around them feels unsteady.

Integrity is the quiet in the noise. It's what brings you home. But integrity doesn't speak for itself.

You can make the right decisions, hold the line, and stay aligned with your values, yet still feel distant to the people you lead if they never experience *who you are* in the process. Integrity determines what you will and won't do. It doesn't automatically let others see what's driving those choices.

That visibility comes from authenticity.

Authenticity is how integrity becomes felt instead of assumed. It's not oversharing or self-expression for its own sake. It's the willingness to show up as a human being, not just a role, so people can trust that your decisions come from something real.

Without authenticity, integrity stays internal. With it, trust becomes relational.

5

Authenticity

When Satya Nadella took over as CEO of Microsoft in 2014, the company wasn't in a great place. The culture was competitive, guarded, and full of people trying to look like the smartest person in the room. Most employees expected Nadella to walk in with the same hard edge: big strategy, big posture, big talk.

Instead, he opened his first all-hands meeting with a story about his son, Zain.

Zain had been born with severe cerebral palsy. Nadella spoke openly about what it was like to become a father under those circumstances and how it forced him to slow down, listen differently, and pay attention to people in ways he hadn't before. He didn't present it as a lesson. He didn't try to spin it into a leadership slogan. He just told the truth.

Then he said something no one expected from a new CEO, "Empathy is not soft... It's essential for innovation."

It changed the entire room.

That moment signaled a shift at Microsoft. The company had been built on intensity and competition. Nadella was offering something different: honesty without armor. He was a leader comfortable being a human first.

Under his watch, Microsoft's culture transformed. People started sharing ideas instead of protecting turf. Feedback mattered. Listening mattered. The company became more creative because the leader at the top wasn't pretending. He understood something simple but rare: people follow the person, not the act.

Authenticity made Nadella more effective because he was trustworthy. And that trust rebuilt a company from the inside out.

My story is quite the opposite. For years, I thought I was doing the right thing, keeping order, keeping peace, keeping face. In truth, I was playing roles. At work, I played the part of the strong, unshakable officer; at home, I tried to be the tough, capable husband, supposedly "providing and protecting." Both versions were partial truths. Neither was whole.

I wasn't lying, but I wasn't living honestly either. With my team, I put on a confident face even when I felt uncertain. With my then-wife, I hid behind a mask when I was struggling. The mask started as protection, a way to stay dependable, but over time, it turned into distance. When you spend too long managing how you're seen, you start to forget who you really are.

The gap between who I was and who I performed to be grew wider until it became a wall. My ex-wife's and my marriage lasted ten years, but I stopped being real with her long before it ended. We were good at maintaining the image, not the connection.

When it was over, I realized I hadn't just lost a partner. I'd lost touch with the version of myself that felt grounded and genuine. The uniform, the discipline, and the control had all become armor.

That experience stripped away the illusion that steadiness and authenticity are the same thing. Steadiness keeps you functional; authenticity keeps you human. It's what allows people to know you, not just rely on you.

It showed me that connection, in any setting, requires alignment between what you say, what you feel, and what you do. When those things drift apart, so do the people around you.

That was the beginning of understanding authenticity for me: not as self-expression or vulnerability for its own sake, but as the courage to live the same story privately that you tell publicly.

Rebuilding Through Vulnerability

When the marriage ended, I did what I'd always done: I tried to move on by staying busy. But this time, work didn't fix it. The problem wasn't something I could outwork; it was something I had to face.

For the first time in my life, I stopped trying to perform my way through pain. I went to therapy. I started meditating. Sitting still was harder than any training I'd done. In silence, everything I'd avoided came up: regret, guilt, the weight of pretending to be fine. But slowly, through that practice, I began to see that what I'd called strength had really been fear of being seen.

As I learned to sit with discomfort, I also learned to tell the truth first to myself, then to others. I started talking to my teammates more openly about what was going on in my life. I told them when I needed space, when I was struggling, and when I didn't have all the answers. It felt unnatural at first, but something unexpected happened: I gained trust.

Authenticity became less about how I expressed myself and more about how I created space for others to do the same. When leaders are real, people feel safe to be real, too. That's where the connection begins. It's come to be known as psychological safety. We've all heard about it, but few truly understand it. It's the belief that you can speak openly without fear of judgment or punishment. Authenticity sends that signal. It tells people, "You can bring your full real self here."

I started to understand that authenticity doesn't just humanize a leader; it stabilizes a team. When people sense sincerity, they stop guessing motives. They listen more, share more, and take more responsibility because trust makes risk possible.

Still, authenticity has limits. It's not about oversharing or letting emotions spill unchecked. I learned to share what helped others connect or learn, not everything I felt in the moment. Being open doesn't mean being unfiltered. Authenticity without discipline turns into chaos.

Over time, that balance reshaped how I led and how I lived. When I said family came first, I made it real, shutting down the laptop, coming home, and being present. When I told my team honesty mattered, I modeled it, even when it was uncomfortable.

Those choices built a kind of steadiness that no performance ever could. People trusted me more, not because I was flawless (I wasn't; I'm not!), but because I was consistent. They knew exactly who was walking into the room.

That's what authenticity really is, not a spotlight on your story, but a mirror that helps others see their own.

Authenticity in Leadership

As I said previously, authenticity is what allows real connection to happen. People can tell when you believe what you're saying and when you're performing. They feel it quickly. When something feels off, trust doesn't slowly erode; it drops off almost immediately.

That's why authenticity isn't optional. Without it, discipline, integrity, and learning lose their weight. They may still exist on paper, but they don't land.

Being authentic doesn't mean sharing every emotion or thinking out loud in real time. It means being steady and honest enough that people feel safe around you. When they sense that, they stop managing impressions and start engaging. They speak up. They admit mistakes. They put real effort into the work instead of hiding behind a role.

Authenticity improves performance by reducing some of the fear. Teams move faster when they aren't trying to decode their leader. Communication gets clearer when people know they're getting the same version of you every day, not a different one depending on the room or the pressure.

Trust grows through consistency, not charisma, not personality—just a leader whose words and behavior line up over time.

Authenticity shows up in small moments. It shows up in how you listen, how you respond under stress, and how you treat people who can't offer you anything in return. It isn't dramatic. It's steady. And that steadiness builds trust long before any crisis puts it to the test.

It matters most when things are uncertain: during change, failure, new beginnings, and conflict. In those moments, people aren't looking for confidence theater. They're looking for something real. If they trust who you are, they'll trust what you ask of them.

Authenticity starts with self-awareness, but it becomes leadership when it shows up consistently. That's where the next piece comes in.

Congruence and Clarity

There was a stretch in my life when I kept saying family came first, but my calendar told a different story: late nights, constant emails, and missed dinners. I told myself it was a commitment. In reality, it was avoidance. Work was easier than facing what my absence created.

That's when I learned authenticity is something you live, not declare. Talking about priorities is easy. Living them is not. Congruence is the bridge between the two.

When your actions match your values, things simplify. People know what to expect from you. You know what to expect from yourself. Decisions get clearer because you're not managing two versions of who you claim to be.

Congruence takes discipline. It requires regular self-checks. Do my choices match my intentions? Am I leading the way I say I live? It's not about perfection. It's about noticing when you're off and correcting course.

Over time, alignment builds more credibility than any speech ever could. Words can inspire, but consistency sustains. When people see that your values don't change with the audience, they relax. They know where you stand, and that allows them to stand with you.

Authenticity isn't a license to be careless. Honesty without empathy harms. "Being myself" without integrity creates chaos.

Authenticity isn't just about what's true for you; it's about how that truth lands on others.

Authenticity starts with awareness, but it earns its power through alignment. That's where it becomes trust, and trust becomes influence.

The Freedom of Being Real

Looking back, authenticity was never about finding the right version of myself. It was about letting go of the false ones. For a long time, I thought leadership meant being composed, certain, and always in control. The harder I tried to project that, the more disconnected I became from others and from myself.

Authenticity brought that connection back. Leadership became simpler. I didn't need to project calm. I could be calm. I didn't need to have every answer. I could ask better questions. I didn't need to prove my worth. I was worthy.

When you stop performing, your team can breathe. They don't have to guess your mood or wonder whether it's safe to speak. They trust your presence because it's steady, not staged. That trust becomes the foundation for real performance, the kind built on respect, not fear.

Authenticity also freed me from the illusion of perfection. I used to think composure meant never faltering. Now I see it as staying grounded enough to be honest when things go sideways. Leadership isn't about showing strength all the time; it's about showing humanity every time.

In the DIAL model, authenticity gives heart to discipline, truth to integrity, and humility to learning. It shifts leadership from command to connection. When you lead from that place, influence doesn't need to be forced. It happens naturally because people follow what feels real.

Leadership is alignment between what you expect and what you embody, between how you show up and how others experience you. When those things line up, leadership feels lighter. That ease isn't laziness; it's freedom.

However, authenticity alone isn't enough to keep a leader effective over time.

You can show up honestly, create a connection, and earn trust, and still drift if you stop questioning your assumptions. You can be real with your team and still repeat the same mistakes if reflection never turns into growth. Authenticity reveals who you are, but it doesn't automatically expand who you're becoming.

That's where learning enters.

Learning is what keeps authenticity from becoming static. It's the willingness to examine your thinking, invite feedback that challenges you, and adjust even when your identity feels attached to the way you've always led. Without learning, authenticity can quietly turn into comfort. With it, authenticity stays alive, adaptive, and relevant.

6

Learning

If you want to understand what real learning looks like, watch the Blue Angels after a flight. The Blue Angels are the Navy's flight demonstration squadron. They're some of the best pilots in the world, flying inches apart at high speed. Their shows get all the attention, but the real work happens afterward.

When they land, they file into a room, sit down together, and begin a brutally honest debrief. Rank disappears. Ego disappears. Nobody performs for the room. One by one, they call out their own mistakes—not someone else's.

"I was off by two feet on the exit."

"I came in high on the break."

"My timing was half a second late."

No excuses. No defensiveness. And when they finish, they end with the same phrase: "Glad to be here."

Feedback is a privilege, and improvement is the expectation. Learning isn't optional if you want to stay on that team.

I love how simple this is. No one waits for a crisis. No one pretends they flew perfectly. They treat learning as part of the job. It's as routine as fueling the jet. That mindset is what keeps them sharp, keeps them alive, and keeps them improving even at a level where most people think improvement is no longer possible.

That's the heart of this chapter. Learning is the willingness to see clearly, adjust honestly, and get a little better every time you touch the ground.

I have spent most of my adult life watching leaders walk into rooms in different ways. Some entered with their shoulders high and their answers ready, determined to prove they were the smartest person in the room. Others walked in differently. They stepped through the door with confidence but also with humility. Their eyes were scanning the room. They asked questions and listened before they spoke. They were not trying to impress anyone. They were trying to understand.

Those were always the people I trusted—not the ones who barked orders or filled every silence with their voice. They were the ones asking the most thoughtful questions. They were the ones who looked around the room during a mission brief and said, "What am I missing?" They were the ones who went to the youngest operator on the team and asked for input because they knew expertise does not always correlate with rank, age, or time in the Teams.

I remember sitting in a room once where an operation was being briefed. Half the room nodded along as if everything made perfect sense. Then one of the senior leaders leaned back in his chair and said, "Walk me through that again. I am not sure I get it." The energy in the room changed instantly. You could see the relief on people's faces.

His willingness to pause and seek clarity gave everyone else permission to be honest.

That is what curiosity does. It opens the door to better information. It makes the team smarter. It makes the leader human (authenticity).

Leadership begins to erode the moment you believe you have to know everything. Learning begins the moment you are willing to admit you do not.

And that is where this chapter starts: with the leader who walks in curiously, the one who listens twice as much as they speak, the one who is not performing certainty but practicing discovery, and the one who, by asking questions, shows his team that he is there to learn with them, not above them.

Because the truth is simple, the leaders we follow most willingly are not the ones with all the answers. They are the ones who never stop learning.

Learning as a Way of Being, Not an Achievement

Some people treat learning like a box to check. They finish a degree, complete a course, read a handful of leadership books, and decide they are done. They think knowledge works like a badge. Once you have it, you just carry it around and flash it when needed.

Leadership does not work that way. Neither does learning. You don't arrive. You don't graduate from it. You don't reach a point where you can say, "I know enough now."

Learning is a way of being, a way of seeing the world, a way of getting up every day and asking, "What can I understand better?"

I mentioned the two types of leaders I've seen before in this context; they both have names in my book: the know-it-alls and the learn-it-alls.

The know-it-alls are easy to spot. They speak first and most. They defend their expertise. They avoid situations where they might be exposed as not knowing something. They shape their identity around being the smartest person in the room, even if that means shutting down the rest of the room. Their focus is on being right. They want to look good.

Then there are the learn-it-alls. These leaders focus on understanding. They are less interested in proving themselves and more interested in growing themselves. They ask better questions—or at least *ask* questions. They invite differing opinions. They listen longer. They trade ego for expansion, and it shows up in every conversation.

One protects an image.

The other strengthens the mind.

It was almost always obvious who belonged in which category. The know-it-alls spent more energy defending their position than improving it. The learn-it-alls may have started behind the know-it-alls, but they improved with every mission and ended up ahead because they were willing to examine their blind spots. They were the ones who came into debriefs saying, "Here is what I think I missed," or "I want to hear what you saw from your angle."

They were not being self-deprecating. They were aware.

Awareness says, "I have strengths, but I also have limits. Help me see what I cannot."

Self-deprecation says, "I will put myself down, so others think I am humble."

Only one of those leads to growth. (And let's be honest, the other one isn't authentic and can be seen from a mile away.)

When you live as a learn-it-all, you stop protecting your identity as an expert and start expanding your capacity as a leader. You stop gripping so tightly to being right and start becoming someone who can adapt to whatever comes next.

And something powerful happens when leaders operate this way. Their people stop hiding. They stop posturing. They stop pretending they understand something when they do not. They start asking better questions, offering better information, and contributing more honestly.

That is when teams become sharper and more aligned. Learning is not about accumulating and hoarding facts. Learning is about cultivating awareness. It is about staying open, curious, and grounded enough to evolve.

A leader who learns sees the world differently. They see every conversation as data. They see mistakes as instruction. They see challenges as invitations. They see their team not as followers, but as teachers.

If leadership had a heartbeat, it would be learning. Without it, everything else grows stale.

The Half-Life of Expertise

There was a time when expertise lasted a lifetime. You could learn a skill, master a trade, or build a career on a set of principles that would hold steady for decades. That world is gone.

Today, the pace of change is so fast that knowledge ages in dog years. What you understood five years ago might be irrelevant now. In some fields, what you learned last year is already outdated.

The half-life of something is the amount of time it takes for something to decay halfway. Expertise works the same way. What we know slowly loses relevance unless we continually update, apply, and refine it.

If leaders rely on static knowledge to guide them, they fall behind—often without realizing it. Some of the most dangerous leaders I have seen were not the inexperienced ones. The dangerous ones were the leaders who relied on old expertise in a new environment. They believed their past success guaranteed future relevance. They did not realize the game had changed.

Tactics evolved. Technologies updated. Enemies adapted. A leader who assumed yesterday's playbook would work tomorrow put people at risk.

I have also seen this play out in the corporate world. Someone who had the answers ten years ago can suddenly become the bottleneck today—not because they lost intelligence or discipline, but because they stopped learning.

But here's the good news: while knowledge expires quickly, the desire to learn never does. That is the real competitive advantage now. Not what you know, but your ability to grow. Not your expertise, but your adaptability. Not your mastery, but your momentum.

This is why the learn-it-all mindset matters. A learn-it-all leader understands that mastery is temporary, but learning is permanent.

They approach every new challenge with the question: What is changing here? What do I need to unlearn? What does this moment require that my old knowledge cannot give me?

Leadership stiffens when learning stops. It stays alive when learning continues. You do not have to stay ahead of everything, but you must stay engaged. You do not need to master every new trend, but you must stay open. You do not need to know what tomorrow holds, but you must remain a learner so you can meet tomorrow when it arrives.

Expertise fades. Curiosity does not.

That is why learning has become one of the most essential dimensions of leadership today.

Curiosity in Action

If you've ever seen the show *Ted Lasso*, you know Ted, the main character, isn't your typical coach. He's an American football coach hired to lead an English Premier League soccer team, even though he knows basically nothing about soccer. It's played for laughs at first, but there's a moment early on when the joke fades, and the truth comes through.

Instead of hiding what he doesn't know, Ted leans into it. He asks questions. He listens. He shows curiosity instead of pretending to be an expert. And the crazy thing is that it works. His willingness to learn builds trust with a team that expected him to fake confidence. His curiosity becomes his advantage.

That's the part of the show that always sticks with me. It's a reminder that curiosity isn't weakness; it's a capacity. Leaders get in trouble not when they don't know something, but when they act on what they do know.

Curiosity is one of the most valuable tools a leader can have. It isn't a speech about growth or a slogan on a wall. It shows up in small, daily choices: how you listen, what you notice, the questions you ask, and whether you're willing to look at reality as it is instead of how you hope it looks.

Curiosity starts with real listening, the kind where you let people finish their thoughts, let silence do some of the work, and give the room enough space for the real story to surface. When you listen like that, you learn what reports never show: tension, misalignment, brilliance, unspoken fears, and who's actually carrying the load.

Observation sharpens that even more. Pay attention to how people act under pressure, how they treat others when no one "important" is watching, and how they respond when plans fall apart. Those moments reveal more about character and capability than any résumé ever could.

Formal training matters, but most learning happens through conversations, mistakes, watching others, and noticing what most people overlook. Some leaders collect information. Curious leaders collect insight—the stories, angles, and perspectives that help them see the full picture.

However, curiosity does have a limit. Every leader has felt it. Looking for one more detail, one more angle, one more confirmation, until you're not learning anymore, you're stalling. That's analysis paralysis. From the outside, it looks like diligence. On the inside, it's avoidance.

Curiosity is productive when you know there's more to know and knowing it will improve the outcome. It becomes a trap when you use it to delay action.

In environments where hesitation has real consequences, you learn quickly that waiting for perfect information is a luxury. You ask the questions that matter, get clear where clarity is essential, and then you move—not because you're certain but because you trust your preparation and your ability to adjust as reality shifts.

Leadership rarely gives you certainty. It gives you moments where you choose to step forward anyway.

Teams pay attention to how you navigate those moments. They watch how long you stay in the question and when you decide to act. They feel the steadiness of a leader who stays curious without losing momentum. They also feel the drift when curiosity becomes an escape hatch from commitment.

When leaders model this kind of curiosity, open-minded but decisive, teams start thinking more broadly and acting more boldly. They learn that mistakes are part of motion, and refinement comes through movement, not endless preparation.

Curiosity keeps you humble, adaptive, and honest. It pulls you closer to the truth, and truth is the foundation of good decisions.

Curiosity opens your eyes, and decision-making moves your feet. Leadership requires both.

Learn From Every Direction

One of the biggest mistakes leaders make is believing that learning only happens from the top down, that wisdom flows in one direction, and that you look to people who are older, more experienced, or more senior to show you the way. There is value in that, of course. But if that is the only place you look, you cut yourself off from half the learning available to you.

Great leaders learn from both ends of the spectrum: the seasoned mentors and the younger generation. They offer different kinds of intelligence, and you need both if you want to stay relevant.

There is something irreplaceable about the wisdom of people who have been through things you have not. They have context. They have scars. They have lived through mistakes, consequences, and victories you might not even be able to imagine yet. When they speak, they are not reciting theory. They are speaking from experience.

I have learned lessons from older mentors that I could never have picked up from a book, no matter how many I read.

However, just as important is the humility to learn from those who are younger. Too many leaders overlook this. They assume wisdom only comes with age or tenure. But younger generations bring something different. Their worldview is not shaped by the same assumptions. They see possibilities where older leaders see obstacles. They ask questions no one else thinks to ask. They understand technology, communication, and culture in ways that can completely reshape how a team operates.

I learned this lesson clearly during a close-quarters battle (CQB) training exercise in the "kill house" with my second platoon. We were running a live-fire iteration, moving fast, heart rates high, doing what we had done dozens of times before. I was the platoon commander—somewhat experienced (though there were guys far more experienced than I), confident, and responsible for the call. I made the call to clear the next room. We stacked on a door. It felt right. It matched the plan. It matched the reps.

Then one of the youngest guys in the platoon, one of the least experienced on paper, spoke up from the stack—calm, direct, no hesitation.

"Hold short, clear long."

What he was telling us was to post security on the near door and clear the hallway and the open room at the far end first. He had seen something I hadn't: a line of sight, a shadow, a geometry problem created by angles and dead space. Or maybe he had simply been trained recently enough that the danger was fresh in his mind instead of assumed away.

I paused, listened, and trusted him.

He was right.

If we had cleared the nearby room first, we would have exposed ourselves to a fatal funnel from the long room down the hall. The kind of mistake that looks obvious in a debrief and unforgivable in real life. That young teammate didn't save us because of rank or experience. He saved us because he was paying attention and because he felt safe enough to speak up.

I remembered that lesson from then on. It sharpened my understanding of leadership. The best decision in that room did not come from the most senior voice. It came from the clearest set of eyes.

I have learned a lot from younger teammates, and even more from my kids. There is a different clarity in how they see the world. They ask questions that cut through the noise. They have a natural honesty that adults often lose. And when you pay attention, you start to see parts of yourself reflected at you—sometimes, the parts you need to work on.

Knowledge flows in all directions, not just downward or upward. It moves sideways, too. You learn from peers. You learn from teammates. You learn from people whose background is nothing like yours. You learn from the specialist sitting three desks away or the new hire who is experiencing everything with fresh eyes.

When you allow yourself to learn from every direction, you become a better listener, a better mentor, and a better human being. You begin to understand that leading is not about standing at the front. It is about staying connected to the whole.

A leader who only learns from above grows slowly. A leader who learns from all around grows exponentially.

That is what keeps you adaptable. That is what keeps you grounded. And that is what keeps you from becoming the leader who is stuck defending the past instead of shaping the future.

Humility as the Gateway to Learning

Humility is the doorway to growth. Without humility, learning becomes impossible because humility requires one simple admission: I do not know everything.

Those five words sound harmless, but for many leaders, they feel like a threat. They believe their value lies in having answers. They assume authority depends on certainty. They worry that vulnerability will cause others to question their competence.

In reality, the opposite is true.

In the book *The Boy, the Mole, the Fox, and the Horse,* written and illustrated by Charlie Mackesy, the boy asks a horse he has befriended, "What's the bravest thing you ever said?"

The horse replies, "Help. Asking for help isn't quitting. It's refusing to quit."

That line captures what humility is in leadership. It is not surrender. It is commitment. It is the decision to keep moving forward without pretending you have it all figured out.

Humility strengthens leadership. Pride weakens it.

Fake humility shows up as self-deprecation, exaggerated modesty, or fishing for reassurance. It looks soft on the surface but is still driven by ego.

Real humility is different. It is the clear awareness that no matter how much you know, your perspective is incomplete. It is the recognition that there is always more to learn and that someone else may see what you cannot. Humility opens space. It lowers defenses. It invites truth.

You see this most clearly in high-stakes environments. During debriefs, the leaders who learn the fastest are never the ones pretending they got everything right. They are the ones who walk into the room open. They review the mission honestly. They admit mistakes quickly. They ask for other perspectives. They look for blind spots rather than hiding from them.

Those debriefs only work because of humility. When ego walks into the room, learning walks out.

Humility also creates psychological safety. When a leader shows they are willing to be wrong, others feel safer telling the truth. People stop sugarcoating. They stop withholding. They stop managing your reactions. They start contributing with honesty and clarity. That kind of environment sharpens teams and improves decisions.

You can feel the difference in how people speak when they know you listen without defensiveness. You can feel the difference in how people think when they know they won't be punished for a new idea. You can feel the difference in how people show up when they know their voice matters.

Humility is strength under control. It is the confidence to stop protecting your image and start investing in your growth.

There is nothing fragile about saying, "I was wrong."

There is nothing small about letting someone younger teach you something new. There is nothing unprofessional about being influenced by a better idea.

Humility frees leaders from the exhausting work of pretending. When people see a leader who learns openly, they are encouraged to do the same.

If learning is the engine of leadership, humility is the ignition. Nothing moves without it.

Stepping Into Discomfort: The Lessons Only Experience Gives

Some lessons only reveal themselves once you leave the familiar. Growth does not come from rehearsing what you already know. It comes from entering situations where you have no choice but to stretch.

For a long time, I avoided skiing, not because I disliked the idea, but because I did not want to be bad at it. I knew it would take me a while to find my balance, and I did not enjoy the thought of looking uncoordinated while everyone else, including kids, glided past me. (I learned to ski twice—once at twenty-eight and again as a forty-year-old!)

Eventually, I agreed to give it a try, and yes, I fell plenty of times. I was nowhere near graceful. But I walked away surprised by how much I enjoyed it. I had let the fear of feeling unskilled keep me from something that turned out to be fun. And I'm still bad, but I do it anyway.

Leaders do this more often than they admit.

They stay inside what they already do well. They take the roles they know how to perform. They avoid situations that might take a toll on their confidence.

The problem is that you cannot grow inside that bubble. New capability always comes from unfamiliar terrain.

Stepping into the unknown is what accelerates growth. You learn new skills quickly because the environment demands it. You operate in situations you've never seen before. You rotate through roles that stretch you in ways you didn't expect. You're pushed past what feels comfortable repeatedly, and each time, you walk away a little more capable than before.

Those experiences taught me something simple: you cannot think your way into growth; you have to move your way into it.

Trying, failing, adjusting, and trying again teaches you more than any amount of planning. You begin to understand where you get stuck, what supports you, what surprises you, and what strengths you did not realize you had.

Not everything you attempt will turn into a talent. That is not the point. The goal is not perfection. It is an expansion. When you allow yourself to be a beginner again, you reopen the part of you that is willing to learn without ego.

Learning Out Loud: Modeling Growth for Your People

Leaders have to show their team that they themselves are still learning—not in a polished, "I read a leadership book this month" way, but in an open and consistent way that people can actually see.

People who lead successful teams share what they are reading, the conferences they attend, the podcasts they listen to, or the experiments they are trying. When leaders make their learning visible, it sends a message to everyone around them: growth is normal here.

People take their cues from the top. If the leader is closed, the team becomes cautious. If the leader is curious, the team becomes engaged. If the leader continues to improve, the team sees improvement as part of the culture.

When you share what you are learning, you create transparency. People see that you are not relying on old experience to carry you. They see that you are sharpening your mind and refining your perspective. That permits them to do the same.

Over time, this shifts the entire environment. Instead of a culture built on expertise alone, you create a culture built on growth. The organization becomes something that evolves instead of something that defends the past. People start to look for insights everywhere, in conversations, failures, feedback, and unexpected moments.

When leaders learn out loud, they show their people that progress is not a private pursuit. It is something shared, practiced, and encouraged. And that is how an organization stops becoming a fixed structure and starts becoming something alive.

The Reframe of a Learning Leader

There is a question I learned to use over the years that changed the way I approach challenges. It is simple, but it shifts everything.

Instead of asking, *Why is this happening to me?*

You ask, *Why is this happening FOR me?*

It is a small change in wording, but a major change in mindset.

The first question puts you in the role of a victim. The second puts you in the role of a student.

One closes you. The other opens you.

I am part of a group where this question comes up often. Someone will share something difficult they are going through: a setback, a conflict, a disappointment. Rather than turning inward with frustration, someone will ask, "What is this trying to teach you?"

The conversation immediately changes. Instead of spiraling into blame or self-criticism, the person begins to look at the situation with curiosity.

A difficult conversation might be teaching you patience. A failure might be teaching you humility. A setback might be teaching you something about timing or preparation. A conflict might be teaching you where you are still reactive.

Nothing becomes wasted when you approach life this way.

I've seen this many times when plans collide with reality. They rarely hold. "No plan survives first contact with the enemy," we say in the military. That "enemy" could be your literal enemy, or it could be something metaphorical. Conditions shift, communications break down, and the unexpected shows up at the worst possible moment. And while it's easy to focus only on the tactical review—what worked, what didn't, what you'd change next time— the deeper conversation is always personal:

What did I learn about myself today?

Where did I fall short?

Where did I hold steady?

Where do I need strengthening?

That mindset is not about perfection. Here again, we see awareness.

When leaders see difficulty as instruction, something powerful happens. They stop fearing the hard moments. They start using them. They seek them. They become more resilient because they are not fighting reality; they are absorbing it. They can face uncertainty without losing stability. They can navigate unexpected changes without panicking. They can recover from mistakes without shame slowing them down.

And when your team sees you respond to challenges with curiosity instead of defensiveness, it becomes contagious. They stop hiding struggles. They stop framing mistakes as personal failures. They begin to see each moment as part of the learning process.

When you adopt this reframing, life becomes less about getting everything right and more about getting everything useful. Even the difficult chapters become meaningful. Even the losses give direction. Even the setbacks contribute to your strength.

Three Rules for Learning as a Leader

After all the conversations, missions, and lessons I have lived through, my approach to learning as a leader comes down to three simple rules. They are not complicated, but they are powerful when practiced consistently.

1. **Stay humble**

    Humility is the foundation of learning. It keeps you aware of your limits and open to better ideas. When you stay humble, you stop pretending you have all the answers. You invite other perspectives. You remain grounded enough to see where you still need to grow.

    Humility keeps your ego small and your awareness wide.

2. **Stay curious**

    Curiosity keeps leadership alive. It prevents you from getting stuck in old patterns or relying on outdated expertise. It pushes you to ask better questions, challenge assumptions, and keep exploring.

    Curiosity is what helps you evolve instead of repeat.

3. **Share what you learn**

    Learning becomes more powerful when you pass it on. When you talk about what you are reading, the lessons you have pulled from mistakes, or the insights you gain from others, it makes growth part of the culture. It encourages the people around you to keep expanding themselves, too.

    Leaders who share their learning strengthen teams that learn alongside them.

These three rules are simple, but they shape everything. They help you stay relevant in a changing world. They keep your mind flexible. They keep your leadership human. And they remind you that leadership is not a performance; it is a continual process of paying attention, adjusting, and growing.

Learning is what keeps leadership alive, but it does something even more important: it keeps the other dimensions honest.

Learning reveals when discipline has hardened into rigidity.

It exposes when integrity has turned into self-justification.

It shows when authenticity becomes comfort rather than growth.

On its own, learning expands perspective. In combination with the other dimensions, it regulates leadership behavior in real time.

Up to now, we've looked at each dimension individually: discipline, integrity, authenticity, and learning.

Each one strengthens leadership in a specific way.

But leadership doesn't happen in isolation.

In practice, these dimensions are constantly interacting. One rises while another recedes. One stabilizes while another challenges. When they work together, leadership becomes fluid rather than rigid and grounded rather than reactive.

That interplay is where leadership either steadies or starts to drift.

And that's where we go next.

7

The Interplay of the Four Dimensions

Every leader brings strengths into the role: discipline, integrity, authenticity, and learning. Each one matters. Each adds value, and none is sufficient on its own.

Leadership also becomes fragile when one of the dimensions quietly drops out of the equation: when discipline advances without integrity, when integrity stands without execution, when authenticity speaks without learning, or when learning accumulates without ownership or action.

The danger isn't leaning too hard. The danger is leading without one of the four.

How the Dimensions Support and Regulate Each Other

On January 28, 1986, the Space Shuttle *Challenger* broke apart seventy-three seconds after liftoff.

Most people remember the explanation that followed: a failed O-ring, cold temperatures, a technical malfunction. That account is accurate but incomplete.

The deeper failure was human. And it remains one of the clearest examples of what happens when leadership dimensions are present but not regulating one another.

The night before the launch, engineers from Morton Thiokol warned NASA leadership that the unusually cold weather posed a serious risk. The data wasn't perfect, but the concern was real. They asked for a delay. They explained what they knew and what they didn't.

Discipline was present, but there was a launch schedule—public pressure, political pressure, a system designed to execute, and, unfortunately, a system destined to eventually fail.

What was missing was integrity to protect dissent, authenticity to make uncertainty safe, and learning that was allowed to influence the final decision.

Somewhere along the way, the question shifted from "Is this safe?" to "Can you prove it's unsafe?" Momentum replaced judgment. The system moved forward not because confidence increased, but because resistance disappeared—eerily similar to my experience with Operation Red Wings.

Seventy-three seconds later, seven astronauts were gone.

The *Challenger* disaster was caused by discipline operating *without* the other dimensions present to restrain it.

That's the danger.

Leadership often fails when one or more dimensions are missing. On the surface, the system still looks functional. In reality, it's unstable.

Each dimension can carry weight for a while. But without all four regulating one another, pressure eventually exposes the gap.

DIAL Without Discipline (Integrity + Authenticity + Learning, Without Execution)

When discipline is missing, values are clear, conversations are open, reflection is happening, people feel heard, and learning is active. However, nothing reliably lands, decisions drift, timelines stretch, accountability diffuses, and follow-through becomes inconsistent.

Integrity is spoken about. Authenticity is expressed. Learning is ongoing. Yet execution lags just enough to matter.

This failure mode emerged clearly at Boeing after the first 737 MAX crash in 2018.

In the aftermath, leadership emphasized safety, responsibility, and doing the right thing. There was real concern inside the organization. Engineers, executives, and board members understood the gravity of what had occurred.

Investigations were launched, and reviews were conducted. Learning was happening, but disciplined execution was missing.

Critical safety changes moved slowly. Accountability remained spread across teams and regulators. Training and design corrections took longer than the situation demanded. The organization acknowledged the problem, but the system didn't move with the urgency it deserved.

Integrity was present.

Authenticity was present.

Learning was present.

Discipline was not.

Months later, a second crash occurred.

This was a failure to operationalize values under pressure. Without discipline, the other three dimensions couldn't translate concern into action. And the cost of that delay was catastrophic.

DIAL Without Integrity (Discipline + Authenticity + Learning, Without Moral Constraint)

When integrity is missing, leadership can still look energetic and effective. Systems are tight. Goals are clear. Communication feels open. Feedback flows. Learning is constant. People know what success looks like.

But the question should quietly disappear.

This is what happened at Wells Fargo.

Aggressive sales targets were enforced relentlessly. Performance was tracked with precision. Coaching was ongoing. Processes were refined. The organization was learning how to sell more efficiently. Leaders communicated frequently and clearly.

What was missing was integrity.

As pressure increased, employees began opening accounts that customers never requested simply to survive. The system rewarded outcomes without guarding ethics. Over time, millions of unauthorized accounts were created.

Discipline drove behavior.

Authenticity kept people engaged.

Learning optimized the system.

Integrity was absent.

Short-term results masked long-term damage. Trust eroded quietly, then all at once. Without integrity, the other dimensions didn't fail; they *accelerated* the harm.

DIAL Without Authenticity (Discipline + Integrity + Learning, Without Human Connection)

When authenticity is missing, policies are followed. Values are upheld. Decisions align with the principle and the system's function.

But people don't feel seen.

Communication becomes formal. Language becomes procedural. Leaders speak accurately, but not humanly. Over time, teams stop bringing concerns forward, not because they don't exist, but because it doesn't feel safe or worthwhile to raise them.

This dynamic was visible during another airline's example: The United Airlines Flight 3411 incident in 2017.

When a passenger was forcibly removed from an overbooked flight, United's initial leadership response focused on policy compliance. Public statements emphasized that employees had followed established procedures. From a technical standpoint, that was true.

From a human standpoint, it missed the moment entirely.

Integrity was present.

Discipline was present.

Learning would eventually follow.

Authenticity was missing.

The language minimized the passenger's experience. The tone sounded detached. Leadership led with rules instead of empathy. Trust eroded rapidly, not because principles were violated, but because humanity was absent.

Only later did leadership shift its response, acknowledging the harm directly and apologizing in human terms. However, by then, credibility had already been damaged.

Without authenticity, leadership becomes "correct" but cold.

DIAL Without Learning (Discipline + Integrity + Authenticity, Without Adaptation)

When learning is missing, leadership often feels confident and grounded. Values are clear. Execution is strong. Communication feels real. The organization knows who it is and how it operates.

But it stops adapting.

Assumptions go unchallenged. Feedback is filtered. New information is treated as noise. Leaders defend what has worked instead of examining whether it still fits.

This pattern played out at Theranos, a Silicon Valley health-technology startup that became infamous for one of the largest fraud scandals in modern business history.

Theranos claimed it had invented a revolutionary blood-testing technology that could run hundreds of medical tests from just a few drops of blood taken from a finger prick. The promise of faster, cheaper, less painful testing attracted massive hype.

The company was founded in 2003 by Elizabeth Holmes, who became a celebrated tech icon. Theranos raised over $700 million, partnered with major retailers like Walgreens, and was valued at nearly $9 billion at its peak.

The problem: the technology never worked as advertised.

Most tests were secretly run on traditional lab machines, while the proprietary devices either malfunctioned or produced unreliable results. Whistleblowers, investigative journalists, and regulators eventually exposed the deception.

Elizabeth Holmes had presented herself as open, mission-driven, and deeply committed to transforming healthcare. She communicated passionately. She framed the company's work as morally significant. To many, she appeared authentic and values driven.

What was missing was learning anchored to reality. Internal warnings were dismissed. Data that contradicted the narrative was ignored or hidden. Curiosity narrowed instead of expanding.

Discipline pushed the vision forward.

Authenticity made it compelling.

Integrity was *claimed* but never tested against evidence.

But learning was completely absent.

When investigative reporting exposed the gap between claims and reality, trust collapsed. Partnerships dissolved. Patients were put at risk. The company unraveled.

Without learning, authenticity became performance. Integrity became rhetoric. Discipline became insistence. The system held together until it didn't.

The Pattern (What Breaks First and Why This Isn't About Missing Everything)

In every leadership failure I've seen, the breakdown happened because at least one dimension disappeared, and the remaining ones continued operating without regulation.

This section is about failure mechanics, not leadership style.

The DIAL model identifies a repeatable pattern: when even one dimension drops out, the others don't compensate; they destabilize.

I've watched moments where gathering more data felt safer than deciding, where good intentions lingered without execution, and where confidence persisted without curiosity. These weren't different problems. They were the same structural failure showing up through different symptoms.

The issue was never intelligence or effort. It was a missing regulator.

Miss one dimension and the system wobbles. Miss it long enough and pressure does the rest.

DIAL without ONE Dimension

Discipline Missing	Integrity Missing	Authenticity Missing	Learning Missing
– Decisions Drift	– Ethics Erode	– Trust Erodes	– Insight Stalls
– Execution Fails	– Morality Fades	– Connection Dries Up	– Growth Ends

The System, Not the Pieces (What the Dimensions Do When They're All Present)

Earlier, we looked at what happens when one dimension goes missing. Now we shift the lens to see why they can't stand alone in the first place.

Discipline provides structure.

Integrity provides direction.

Authenticity provides connection.

Learning provides adaptation.

Each one exists to regulate the others, not replace them.

That's why this model is more like a living circuit than a checklist. Each part draws energy from the others, always adjusting to the pressure of people, pace, and reality.

Leaders who endure aren't the ones who never drift. They're the ones who notice early and adjust. The dial just needs calibration.

Reading the Moment Before Choosing a Posture (Diagnosis: What Leaders Assess)

Before choosing how to lead, a leader has to see what they're really looking at. This step isn't about action; it's about perception, about noticing the shape of the moment before deciding how to meet it (again, awareness).

Leadership breaks down most often not because leaders choose the wrong dimension, but because they choose too early, before the environment is clearly understood.

Reading the moment requires leaders to assess a small set of contextual signals that shape what the system will demand next:

- **Urgency**

    What is the required speed of action? High urgency compresses time and narrows tolerance for exploration, often requiring clearer structure and decisive execution. Lower urgency allows space for learning, dialogue, and adjustment.

- **Stakes**

    What is the cost of being wrong? As consequences rise, decisions must be more firmly anchored in values and executed with discipline. Lower-stakes environments permit experimentation without destabilizing trust.

- **Emotional climate**

    What is the current psychological state of the team? Stress may call for steadiness and integrity. Fatigue often requires authenticity and pacing. Widespread uncertainty typically signals the need for learning before action.

- **Team capability**

    How experienced and confident is the group? Highly capable teams can operate with greater autonomy and adaptability. Less experienced teams require clearer structure and direction to stay aligned.

- **Strategic horizon**

  Is the focus on immediate resolution or long-term positioning? Short-term pressure favors discipline and clarity. Long-term objectives demand learning, iteration, and adaptability.

These indicators prevent default behavior. They help leaders resist overusing the dimension that feels most comfortable and instead choose deliberately based on what the moment requires. Diagnosis ensures the leader is responding in the right way to the right one.

Reactive vs. Intentional Switching (Why Timing Matters More Than Balance)

When does the shift actually happen—that moment when a leader moves from one dimension to another?

The difference comes down to whether you're leading the change or being pushed into it.

Reactive switching occurs after failure forces change. The leader adjusts because the current approach stopped working. This creates inconsistency and stress.

Intentional switching happens before the moment demands it. The leader anticipates the shift and proactively adjusts, creating confidence and stability for the team.

The highest form of leadership in the DIAL model is *timing*.

Knowing when to anchor with integrity.

When to impose structure.

When to widen perspective through learning.

When to slow down and reconnect through authenticity.

Distortions and Defaults (Why Strong Leaders Drift Under Pressure)

What does pressure do to that clarity? Pressure doesn't create new behaviors. It amplifies existing ones.

Under stress, leaders default to the dimension that feels safest. What is normally a strength becomes a shortcut. Instead of reading the full context, leaders respond through the lens that gives them control.

This is where distortions emerge:

- Discipline becomes overcontrol
- Integrity becomes image protection
- Authenticity becomes emotional spillover
- Learning becomes hesitation

These distortions happen because *pressure narrows perception,* not because the leaders lack skill.

Early Warning Signs (How Leaders Regain Balance Before Damage Occurs)

Before full-on distortion happens, there are signals:

- Work slows due to re-checking
- Decisions feel heavier than they should
- Communication sharpens or fragments
- Teams self-censor
- Leaders feel the need to justify or defend

None of these signal *failure.* They signal that *default behavior is replacing intentional choice.*

Recognizing these signs early allows leaders to recalibrate before trust erodes or momentum stalls. That moment of noticing before correction is forced is where leadership regains control.

Recurring Patterns of Interplay (Configuration: How the Dimensions Combine)

Once the situation is understood, a different question emerges: *how do the dimensions tend to organize themselves in environments like this?*

Unlike the "Reading the Moment Before Choosing a Posture" section earlier, this section is not about *reading signals*. It is about *recognizing structure*.

Across industries, teams, and contexts, the DIAL dimensions consistently combine in recognizable ways. Certain environments elevate specific dimensions to drive action, while others shift into stabilizing roles to prevent imbalance.

These are not scripts or formulas. They are recurring patterns—reliable configurations that show up whenever similar conditions are present.

1. Crisis Environments

Crisis compresses time and reduces tolerance for ambiguity. Teams need order, clarity, and steadiness.

Primary dimensions:

- **Discipline** to establish structure and decisive pathways
- **Integrity** to anchor decisions as conditions shift rapidly

Supporting dimension:

- **Authenticity** to maintain trust, calm, and human connection

Pattern: The leader establishes order quickly, makes principle-based decisions under pressure, and uses authenticity to reassure the team and regulate emotion. Learning remains present but constrained; the environment rarely allows extended analysis.

2. Long-Term Execution

Sustained work depends on rhythm, consistency, and refinement.

Primary dimensions:

- **Discipline** to maintain standards and routines
- **Learning** to improve methods and identify inefficiencies

Supporting dimension:

- **Integrity** to keep execution aligned with purpose

Pattern: Discipline provides stability, learning drives improvement, and integrity ensures progress doesn't drift from intent. Authenticity appears when motivation or alignment needs reinforcement, not as a constant driver.

3. High-Ambiguity Conditions

Incomplete information requires exploration and adaptability.

Primary dimensions:

- **Learning** to make sense of uncertainty
- **Authenticity** to maintain transparency and steadiness

Supporting dimension:

- **Discipline** to prevent drift

Pattern: Learning frames what is happening, authenticity keeps the team grounded and connected, and light discipline provides enough structure to stay oriented. Integrity remains present as a guardrail but does not dominate the posture.

4. Team Conflict or Interpersonal Tension

Conflict disrupts alignment and trust.

Primary dimensions:

- **Learning** to understand perspectives and root causes
- **Integrity** to ensure fairness and psychological safety

Supporting dimension:

- **Authenticity** to adapt communication and rebuild connection

Pattern: The leader seeks understanding first, responds with consistency and fairness, and adjusts communication to the emotional temperature of the team. Discipline appears as boundary-setting, not control.

5. Growth and Scaling Phases

Expansion demands speed, alignment, and coherence.

Primary dimensions:

- **Authenticity** to create shared meaning during rapid change
- **Integrity** to preserve purpose as pace increases

Supporting dimension:

- **Discipline** to formalize processes as growth stabilizes

Pattern: Authentic communication keeps teams aligned, integrity anchors decisions, and discipline is introduced gradually to prevent chaos. Learning accelerates innovation but does not define the posture.

These all reinforce a central truth of the DIAL system: no environment requires all four dimensions equally. Every situation requires a few primary and relies on one or two others to stabilize the system.

Understanding these configurations allows leaders to anticipate what the moment will demand before imbalance forces correction.

Real World Example of the Four Dimensions' Interplay

In 2018, twelve boys and their soccer coach were trapped deep inside a flooded cave system in northern Thailand. Like millions of others, I followed every update I could find. I read the articles, watched every interview, studied the photos, and when the documentary and the full-length film were released, I watched both. Even knowing the ending, I still found myself sitting on the edge of my seat. Yes, because of the danger, but also because of the continually shifting leadership dynamics.

Most people remember the miracle. Fewer remember the mess that came before it.

In the beginning, it was all ego and turf: Thai Navy SEALs claiming command, local officials managing optics, international teams tiptoeing around hierarchy and culture. And then these civilian British cave divers show up: IT guys, engineers, and doctors.

They were dismissed as outsiders who didn't belong in the chain of command.

Nothing about the early operation was clean. It was human, and that's what made it such a powerful example of leadership.

Slowly at first. Reluctantly. Then decisively.

People let go of pride and stopped fighting over who was in charge. They started asking who was right for the job.

They listened to the ones who knew the caves, even if those were civilians with day jobs in IT and medicine. The real turning point wasn't tactical. It was emotional. Ego gave way to purpose.

From that point forward, the entire mission aligned. Calm replaced chaos. Expertise replaced authority. Humility replaced territorialism. And in the pitch-black of that cave, where breathing had to be slow, deliberate, and controlled, you could see what leadership looks like when everything unnecessary falls away: presence, cooperation, clarity, and courage.

When you look closely, the entire rescue is a masterclass in DIAL leadership.

DISCIPLINE: Doing What Must Be Done, Especially When It's Hard

The cave divers operated in conditions even most elite military operators will never experience: zero visibility, jagged tunnels barely wider than their bodies, unpredictable currents, and the constant risk of hitting their tanks, dislodging masks, or losing the line that guided them out. Every movement had to be deliberate. Every action had to be controlled. One mistake could kill the diver, the child, or both.

Discipline was quiet repetition, practicing until positioning a boy's body, securing a mask, and threading a tight turn became automatic. Every detail dialed in before the first dive.

Discipline isn't just doing hard things. It's doing them precisely when everything screams to rush. That's what kept the boys breathing.

INTEGRITY: Building Trust Others Can Stand On

The lead divers had assessed every alternative. Walking the boys out was impossible. The passages were narrow, winding, and fully submerged. Water levels were unstable. Visibility was near zero. None of the boys could swim. Panic in a confined underwater passage would be fatal. The only viable option was brutally simple yet absolutely terrifying.

Each boy would have to be sedated, fitted with a full-face diving mask, secured to a diver, and guided, unconscious, through hours of submerged cave passages. If a mask failed, if a body snagged, if a diver lost orientation, if a boy awoke from the sedation, there would be no way to resurface, no room to improvise.

That was the method. And the divers told officials, parents, and the world the truth no one wanted to hear: "There is a real chance none of these boys survive. But this is the only method that gives them any chance at all."

They didn't soften it. They didn't promise success. They didn't offer false reassurance to ease the fear in the room. They spoke plainly about the risks, the limits, and the consequences.

That honesty mattered.

Once the truth was fully on the table, everyone involved could consent to reality instead of hope. Decisions were made with eyes open. Expectations were aligned. Trust was formed not because the outcome was guaranteed, but because nothing was hidden.

Integrity in that moment meant carrying the full weight of the truth into every dive, every decision, and every breath taken underwater in the darkness of the cave.

That kind of integrity makes trust possible in the presence of it.

AUTHENTICITY: Leading as a Real Human, Not a Performance

One of the most remarkable leaders in the entire mission was Dr. Richard Harris, the Australian anesthesiologist and cave diver. He didn't look like the stereotypical hero. He was soft-spoken, humble, and deeply human.

But he was the exact person the mission required.

Only someone with his rare combination of cave-diving experience and medical expertise could safely sedate the boys for the extraction. He initially resisted the spotlight, hesitant to take on a role that carried so much risk. But authenticity isn't about seeking responsibility; it's about accepting it when it's yours to take.

His presence—calm, grounded, and unpolished—set the emotional tone for the entire rescue team.

LEARNING: Growing Continuously or Risking Stagnation

The methods that ultimately saved the boys had never been attempted before. No one had ever sedated kids, tied their arms, and floated them face-down through submerged tunnels for hours. Every expert called it impossible—a death sentence.

But the rescuers adapted. They learned aggressively. They listened to specialists. They debated, tested, and recalibrated. They abandoned assumptions that didn't serve the mission and let solutions emerge from curiosity instead of rank.

The Real Lessons

This rescue succeeded because people dialed in their leadership. They let go of ego. They trusted expertise as they explored new options. They stayed disciplined under pressure. They told the truth. They teamed with humility. They let learning, not pride, guide their decisions.

These are the lessons this rescue clearly teaches. And it's why we're talking about it here, because DIALed-in leadership doesn't just apply to combat or business. It applies anywhere the stakes are real and people are counting on you.

When leaders understand how the four dimensions interact, leadership stops feeling mysterious. You can see why things wobble. You can name what's missing. You can feel when one dimension is overpowering the others.

But awareness alone doesn't prevent failure.

The real test comes when pressure enters the room.

As we've discussed earlier, under stress, leaders don't rise to their ideals. They fall back on their defaults. Discipline tightens. Integrity gets rationalized. Authenticity goes quiet or spills out sideways. Learning slows just when it's needed most. The system drifts, the dial slips, one dimension at a time.

This is where leadership stops being theoretical.

Because the consequences of imbalance show up in decisions made too fast or too slow. In silence where there should have been honesty. In confidence that isn't backed by reality. In moments where the cost of missing one dimension becomes painfully clear.

Chapter 8 isn't theory. It's what happens when you ignore the dial.

8

How Leaders Move Between Dimensions

Most leadership moments don't announce themselves with urgency. They show up quietly, mid-conversation, mid-decision, mid-meeting, when the stance you walked in with no longer fits what is unfolding. Nothing is obviously broken. No one has said the wrong thing yet. But internally, you feel it. That internal signal is the moment leadership happens.

In the military, in corporate environments, and in coaching leaders today, most people fail because they lack at least one of the four dimensions discussed previously, *or* because they stay in the wrong one for too long.

They push structure when the team needs space. They slow down to reflect when the moment requires commitment. They keep adapting when clarity is needed. Or they press for momentum when steadiness would restore trust.

The problem is rarely capability. It's timing.

Leadership doesn't live in the dimension you prefer. It lives in the dimension that's needed and your ability to notice and shift.

From Awareness to Action

Many leaders reach a point where they understand themselves well. They can describe their tendencies, name their strengths, and explain how they react under pressure. That awareness matters.

However, awareness alone doesn't change outcomes. It only sharpens the mirror.

The real friction in leadership begins when awareness meets *behavior*. Leaders often recognize that the moment calls for a different stance, yet still fail to adjust in real time. Momentum carries them forward. Habit overrides intention. What is familiar feels safer than what is accurate.

That gap between *knowing* and *doing* is not a character flaw. It is a wiring issue. Understanding something intellectually does not automatically translate into embodied action under pressure.

This is why movement must be practiced, not just understood.

Internal and External Signals

Shifts rarely start with external conflict. They start with signals.

Internal cues are often the earliest indicators that a shift may be needed. They show up as changes in breathing or posture, a rise in urgency or irritation, emotional tightening, narrowing attention, difficulty listening, or the impulse to speed up, shut down, or control the conversation.

These cues don't necessarily mean something is *wrong*. They mean something is *changing*.

External cues reveal what the environment is asking for. The room gets quieter. People hesitate before speaking. Energy dips or tension rises. Work slows. Priorities feel unclear, and conversations loop without progress.

Internal cues reveal your state. External cues reveal the moment.

A shift is needed when those two no longer align with the dimension you're using. That mismatch creates the shift threshold. You feel one thing. The moment asks for another. And your current stance fits neither.

The mistake most leaders make is trying to push through that mismatch. Skillful leaders recognize it early and adjust before the team feels the cost.

The **SHIFT** Protocol

Leaders shouldn't shift quadrants by accident. They ideally shift because they notice something, pause long enough to evaluate it, and then adjust. This is something I've loosely modeled after the military's OODA (oo-dah-loop). This came from fighter pilots—observe, orient, decide, act, and then do it again (hence, "loop"). I call my version the SHIFT Protocol. Like the OODA loop, the SHIFT Protocol gives this process structure. It turns adaptability into a repeatable skill instead of a reactive impulse.

Each step builds on the previous one. Each step slows the leader down just enough to regain accuracy without losing momentum.

S – Sense the Signals

Shifts begin with awareness, and awareness begins with noticing patterns.

Leaders who are DIALed in pay attention to two things: what is happening in the work and what is happening in the people doing the work. Some signals point toward the need for more structure and direction. Others reveal breakdowns in trust or emotional disconnection. Others highlight that the environment has changed and new learning is required.

In practice, this sounds like:

- Confusion or slow execution → Discipline needed
- Doubt or unease about motives → Integrity needed
- Emotional withdrawal or silence → Authenticity needed
- Repetition of old patterns → Learning needed

These signals don't judge the leader. They simply reflect what the moment is asking for.

H – Hold the Pause

Your instincts will always push you toward your most *familiar* dimension. This isn't always the *best* dimension.

The disciplined leader will move to control.

The authentic leader will move to openness.

The learning-oriented leader will gather more information.

The integrity-driven leader will anchor harder in principle.

Holding the pause interrupts that reflex. It's the moment you delay your first reaction long enough to make a proper choice. Maybe your instinct was right. Maybe it wasn't.

The pause doesn't need to be long. It just needs to be deliberate.

A leader who can pause is a leader who can remain accurate.

I – Identify the Gap

Once the pause creates space, clarity becomes possible.

This step is about determining the difference between what the situation *needs* and how you are *currently* leading.

If people are unclear, the gap is discipline.

If people are questioning intent, the gap is integrity.

If people feel unseen, the gap is authenticity.

If the team keeps repeating old mistakes, the gap is learning.

This is where the leader pinpoints misalignment, not in themselves, but between their stance and the environment. Identifying the gap is what prevents shifting in the wrong direction.

F – Flex (No, Not Your muscles!)

Flexing is the intentional adjustment a leader makes to realign with the moment—not a performance, not a personality shift, a practical recalibration.

To flex means choosing actions that belong to the dimension the moment requires.

- Flexing into discipline: Setting priorities, tightening expectations, giving direction people can act on immediately

- Flexing into integrity: Explaining reasoning, clarifying values, or taking responsibility so trust is restored

- Flexing into authenticity: Acknowledging emotions, sharing relevant context, or asking a grounded human question

- Flexing into learning: Inviting feedback, exploring alternatives, or creating a safe path for experimentation.

The key is that flexing isn't theoretical. You make one small, deliberate adjustment that changes the trajectory of the moment. Flexing is movement with intention, not movement for the sake of movement.

T – Test and Tune

Once the adjustment is made, the leader pays attention to whether it worked.

Are people clearer?

Has the tension eased?

Do decisions move forward?

Has the energy shifted?

Does the team feel reconnected?

Is new information coming forward?

If not, the leader makes a second adjustment, often smaller and more precise.

Testing and tuning turn a single shift into continuous calibration. It keeps the leader aligned with the truth of the moment rather than the comfort of their default.

Why the SHIFT Protocol Matters

Leadership environments move fast. Teams move fast. Pressures shift without warning. The SHIFT Protocol gives leaders a way to stay oriented. It replaces instinct with clarity. It ensures that the dimension you *choose* is the one that the moment *requires*. And it teaches you to adjust your stance as conditions evolve.

A leader who can SHIFT becomes steady not because they stay in one place, but because they know exactly when to move.

The Difference Between a Shift and an Overcorrection

Shifting between dimensions is a controlled adjustment. Overcorrecting is a reaction. The two can look similar on the surface, but they produce very different outcomes.

A shift is intentional. It aligns your approach with what the situation genuinely needs.

An overcorrection is emotional. It aligns your behavior with whatever you're trying to escape in the moment: pressure, discomfort, frustration, or fear.

Leaders often confuse the two, especially under stress. They sense something is off, but because they don't pause long enough to identify the need, they swing too far in the opposite direction.

The intent is right, but the execution exaggerates the response.

Signs You're Overcorrecting

Overcorrection reveals itself through imbalance. You'll notice:

- A sudden spike in intensity or control
- Trying to regain order quickly rather than re-establish clarity
- A shift in tone that feels sharper or heavier than the moment demands
- Pushing urgency instead of directing focus
- Oversharing or emotional over-explanation

- Trying to connect so quickly that boundaries are lost
- Endless questioning or analysis
- Mistaking activity for progress
- Rigid values enforcement that feels punitive instead of steadying
- Anchoring to principle instead of leading from it

These aren't leadership adjustments. They are attempts to relieve internal discomfort.

Why Overcorrections Happen

Overcorrections usually happen for one of three reasons. First, stress narrows your field of view. Under pressure, leaders see less. Options shrink. Nuance disappears. Without awareness, you jump from one dimension to another in a sweeping motion instead of a measured shift.

Second, leaders confuse speed with accuracy. Feeling behind or uncertain, they try to make up ground with intensity. Urgency without clarity creates noise, not progress.

Third, habit activates faster than awareness. Even with the DIAL model in mind, the body and emotions move before intention does.

None of these makes someone a bad leader. They show how quickly default patterns take over when pressure rises.

Recovering from an Overcorrection

Correcting an overcorrection doesn't require a drastic reset. It requires a grounded recalibration. Skilled leaders do three things.

First, they re-ground themselves. A brief pause or breath slows the reaction pathway and interrupts emotional momentum.

Second, they revisit the need, not the feeling. They ask, "What does this situation actually require?" rather than "What do I feel pushed to do right now?"

Third, they reset tone or stance clearly but calmly. A small realignment is far more effective than undoing everything.

This is how leaders stay accurate while moving—not by staying still, but by adjusting cleanly, deliberately, and without noise.

A leader who can SHIFT becomes steady not because they stay in one place, but because they know exactly when to move.

What you've just learned is not a formula. It's a way of orienting yourself when leadership moments arrive quietly and leave consequences behind. It's how leaders stay accurate in motion.

But no framework leads for you.

At some point, the diagrams end. The protocols fade into the background. And what remains is you, standing in real moments, deciding how you will show up when there is no clear right answer and no immediate feedback.

That's where leadership lives.

9

Leadership Beyond the Pages

You've come through the full arc of this book, from understanding the four dimensions to seeing how they interact, to learning how to move between them with intention. However, the real work of leadership begins after the final chapter, when there are no prompts, no diagrams, and no structured sections guiding your next step.

Everything you've read so far points to a simple truth that has surfaced repeatedly across my experiences: leadership is already unfolding in your life, whether you claim the title or not. It shows up in how you speak to people, how you handle stress, how you manage conflict, how you listen, and how you follow through on what you said you would do.

These are not dramatic moments. They are quiet, ordinary choices. And over time, they shape your impact far more than any position ever will.

This final chapter isn't here to introduce something new. It's here to bring you back to yourself—to the leader you already are, and the leader you are still becoming.

The DIAL model is a tool. The SHIFT Protocol is a practice. But neither of them matters unless they show up in how you live and lead each day. The purpose of this chapter is to help you cross that threshold where the model becomes less of a reference and more of a rhythm.

This isn't a summary.
It's a pause.

What the Four Dimensions Add Up To

By now, you've spent time inside each of the four dimensions—discipline, integrity, authenticity, and learning—not as concepts but as lived principles.

Each one carries weight. Each one has a purpose. However, the strength of the model was never in any single dimension. It has always been in what they create together.

Taken as a whole, they point toward a way of leading that is clear, steady, and intentional.

Discipline brings structure, focus, and follow-through. Integrity aligns what you believe with what you do. Authenticity brings humanity into the work, and that creates connection. Learning brings curiosity, adaptability, and openness to change.

However, these are not four separate *identities* a leader switches between. They are four expressions of the same underlying commitment: to lead in a way that is grounded, responsible, and present.

Throughout this book, one theme has surfaced repeatedly: leadership is not performance. It is consistency. It's acting in a way that reflects who you intend to be, even when conditions shift, pressure rises, or clarity feels harder to reach. Consistency doesn't mean rigidity. It means having a clear center from which you respond.

The four dimensions give shape to that center. They help you recognize what leadership is asking of you in any given moment: to set direction, to act with principle, to connect as a human being, and to keep learning as the situation evolves.

Together, they form something simple but demanding: a personal standard for how you show up, not one imposed by a role or title but one you choose to carry every day.

The DIAL model doesn't try to create a new version of you. It helps you express the most grounded version that's already there.

Leadership as Daily Practice, Not a Title

I started with this, and I'll end with this: leadership is not granted by rank, position, or authority. It's revealed through how you carry yourself day to day.

You don't become a leader when someone puts you in charge. People put you in charge because you're a leader (well, ideally, anyway). You're a leader in how you listen, how you respond under stress, and how you handle responsibility when no one is assigning it.

This has been true across every part of my life. In the Teams, leadership showed up in actions, not words. In coaching, it appears in whether someone follows through, stays present in hard conversations, or remains steady when others lean on them. And outside of work, it shows up in how you handle frustration, disappointment, and accountability in your closest relationships.

Leadership is already happening. The real question is whether you're paying attention to the moments it reveals itself.

The model you've learned doesn't change that reality. What it does is make those moments visible. It helps you notice the patterns that strengthen your leadership and the habits that quietly undermine it.

Daily leadership lives in tone, attention, and consistency. It's where discipline becomes reliability, integrity becomes alignment, authenticity becomes trust, and learning becomes relevance.

Not through big gestures but through repeated actions that compound over time.

The leaders people trust most aren't the ones who perform leadership. They're the ones who live it. They listen more than they speak. They own mistakes without drama. They stay curious. And they show up the same way whether anyone is watching or not.

That's why DIAL is less about instruction and more about awareness. It guides how you carry yourself when there's no script. It shapes how you respond when the answers aren't obvious. And it influences the presence you bring into rooms that don't come with clear rules.

Leadership becomes real in these small, repeated moments. It's not what you *say* about leadership. It's what you *practice.*

Bringing DIAL Into Your Life and Work

Everything in this book leads to one simple truth: the model only matters if it becomes part of how you move through your daily life—not just at work, not only in high-pressure moments, and not only when you're formally "leading."

The four dimensions show up everywhere—in conversations, expectations, conflict, and the presence you bring to the people around you.

DIAL is not meant to be theoretical. It's meant to help you notice, to see your default tendencies, to recognize when you tighten, rush, withdraw, or hesitate, and to spot the moments when discipline, integrity, authenticity, or learning could shift the tone or direction of what's unfolding.

And along with DIAL, the SHIFT Protocol matters most in moments that don't feel like leadership at all: when you pause before responding, when you ask what the situation actually needs, and when you adjust with intention rather than react from habit.

This isn't about getting it right every time. It's about noticing. Noticing where you naturally lean. Noticing where you resist shifting. Noticing which signals you overlook. Noticing the difference it makes when you choose response over reaction.

The invitation here is simple: bring more awareness into who you already are and let the model sharpen how you move through the world. Over time, that awareness becomes instinctive. It shapes how you think, how you communicate, and how you set the tone around you.

Leadership lives in ordinary moments.

DIAL helps you meet them with purpose.

Closing Reflection: The Legacy You Leave in Small Moments

Leadership is often described in grand, powerful-sounding terms like vision, influence, and impact. However, as you've seen throughout this book, it is actually way simpler than that.

People remember how you showed up in moments that didn't look like leadership at all. They remember whether you listened, whether you followed through, whether they felt steadier or more unsettled after speaking with you, whether your presence clarified or complicated things, and whether you acted from principle when it mattered.

Those small moments become your legacy long before anyone talks about accomplishments or credentials.

DIAL isn't here to turn you into someone else. It's here to support the version of you that leads with awareness and intention—the version people trust because your behavior matches your values.

Legacy isn't built at the end of a career. It's built today—in conversations, in decisions, in moments you choose clarity over comfort, and in pauses where you respond with the presence the situation deserves.

You may never know which small moment made the difference for someone. That's the nature of leadership.

Its impact is often invisible but always felt.

As you move beyond these pages and back into your environments, the question isn't whether you understand the model. It's simpler than that:

What mark will your leadership leave next?

That is the work now, and it's already in your hands.

About the Author

Jon Macaskill is a retired US Navy SEAL Commander, leadership consultant, speaker, and mindfulness teacher. Over the course of his military career, he led and trained teams in high-pressure, high-stakes environments where clarity, discipline, and emotional control weren't optional; they were the difference between mission success and failure.

Today, Jon brings those same principles to leaders, organizations, and families. He is the founder of Focus Now Training, a performance and attention training company that helps teams reduce distraction, improve decision-making, strengthen communication, and operate with greater situational awareness. His work blends elite military leadership experience with neuroscience, mindfulness, and practical leadership tools designed for the real world.

Jon is also the co-host of the *Men Talking Mindfulness* podcast, where he explores leadership, mental fitness, fatherhood, resilience, and modern masculinity through honest conversations with high performers across industries.

He is the author of *Unleashing Inner Strength: A Navy SEAL's Guide to Preparedness, Resilience, Grit, and Compassion Through Mindfulness*, in which he shares lessons from combat, command, and civilian life, emphasizing that true strength is built not just through toughness but through awareness, integrity, and compassion.

Jon lives with his wife and three children and is passionate about helping people lead with presence at work and at home.

To learn more about Jon's speaking, leadership training, and executive coaching, visit FocusNowTraining.com or connect with him on LinkedIn. If you're ready to improve focus, performance, and resilience inside your organization, schedule a discovery call to explore working together.